Finding Yesterday One Memory At A Time

By
Mary Anne Tuck

ISBN 978-1-63784-275-1 (paperback)
ISBN 978-1-63784-276-8 (digital)

Hawes & Jenkins Publishing
16427 N Scottsdale Road Suite 410
Scottsdale, AZ 85254
www.hawesjenkins.com

Printed in the United States of America

Finding Yesterday
One Memory At A time

MEMORIES OF A LIFETIME

Life At Hidden Meadows Farm

Banished But Not Forever

Remembering Ann

A Gift To Be Shared

MEMORIES OF LIFE

Every day, memories of life invade my mind. *"I'm going to write it down"*, I say.
But I don't.
Today is a good day to begin.
Funny how and why, incidents pop into your mind that really are of no substance,
but for some reason, you remember.

Memories from my childhood are about sunshine, green grass, playing outside and
being happy. No clouds, no rain, no snowstorms, although I do remember playing
in the snow and sliding down the snow covered hill next to our garage, on a piece of
cardboard. That was fun. Driving by my childhood house and the hill nearby just
the other day, I noticed it wasn't there; except in my memories.
That's ok.
At least I have them with me all the time.

Banished But Not Forever

*"I don't remember what it was I said one day. I must confess, from a very young age I was prone
to say things without thinking. Whatever it was, it offended (her). I was banished from the farm
for a year when I was twelve."*

What a wonderful lady!

Mr. and Mrs. Kelly and their family came to be caretakers of the County Farm,
across the road from my childhood home in the forties. I was ten years of age when
the Kelly family came to live in our neighborhood.

I adored the majestic building, easily seen from our front yard.

The farmhouse was a very large, very old building. Elderly folks who couldn't
afford a home and needed someone to care for them, came there to live.

Some folks called it the Poor Farm, but to me, it was never poor.

It always displayed a dignity which deserved the regal title, "County Farm".

When I was very young, I began to visit the Farm as often as I could. There were
seven older people living there at the time. A section of the large house was set

2

aside for their comfort; a dining room, bedrooms, a bath and a living room. There were bedrooms upstairs. I never saw them, but I knew where the doorway to the stairs was located in a hallway.

Mrs. Kelly cooked the meals for the residents. She baked, canned and prepared what appeared to me to be wonderful food.

One of the more able ladies who lived at the Farm, whose name was "Rilla", helped with the table settings of the long dinner table in their separate dining room. She always turned plates and cups at each place upside down before the meal; first the plate, then the cup.

I was fascinated by Rilla's table arrangement. I'd never seen anything like it.

Mother wasn't happy when I tried to set our dinner table the same way.   It seemed quite picturesque to me.   I could never understand Mother's disdain for the arrangement. Perhaps she wasn't against it, she just knew we didn't have a need for it.

On the front side of the house, which I passed on my way to visit with Mrs. Kelly, there was a porch. The older ladies often sat in their rocking chairs, watching the world (and me) go by.

On one such occasion, I noticed one of the ladies had a newspaper spread out across her stomach as she sat quietly in her chair. I asked her why she had it there and she said, "It's to keep my bowels warm".

Now that's a remedy I would never have thought of on my own.

The Kelly family had a grown son and daughter pursuing careers in far off parts of the country. Their youngest daughter still lived at home and was soon to graduate from high-school.

I don't remember what it was I   said one day. I must confess, from a very young age I was prone to say things without thinking. Whatever it was, it offended Mrs. Kelly.   I was banished from the farm for a year when I was twelve.

It was to be a lifelong lesson.

Be careful what you say. Be aware, if you can, of how the other person may be receiving your words.

For the next year, I didn't follow my favorite path to the County Farm.   At thirteen I ventured a return.

Mrs. Kelly welcomed me as before.   Our friendship continued.

Many times I watched Mrs. Kelly kneading a very large pan of bread dough in the County Farm kitchen.   I now bake my own bread and would never be able to knead such an amount of dough at one time; although now, as an adult, I am a larger woman than Mrs. Kelly; but apparently not as strong.

My bread recipe dictates kneading the dough for ten minutes.   I'm sometimes able to continue for seven. Mrs. Kelly would likely suggest that the bread would be finer if I followed the directions of the recipe.

(She was strong and determined with many responsibilities in life.   She always had time for me.)

When visiting at just the right time, the aroma of baking bread always greeted me near the kitchen door.   Not far behind me, there were bread customers waiting to purchase a wonderful loaf of Mrs. Kelly's homemade bread.

As I recall, she charged them $1.00 per loaf; the loaves were huge. I checked with the Bureau of Labor Statistics and found that one dollar in the 1940's is equal to $16.24 in 2022.   With that in mind, Mrs. Kelly's customers were willing to pay a rather high amount for her bread; at that time. (Something to reflect upon.)

It was worth it!

Her long gray hair, was always carefully braided and wrapped neatly around Mrs. Kelly's head. A clean and ironed cotton dress was always her attire.

She never walked anywhere slowly; always on the move and carrying out her vast responsibilities.

The kitchen and her family's living quarters were neat and very clean. The dishes were done and everything was in its' place.   In the pantry, next to the kitchen, sat a wire basket of eggs, waiting for her local customers who weekly purchased the freshest eggs in town.

Sometimes Mrs. Kelly allowed me to go to the chicken coop with her, to gather the eggs. I loved it.

One summer, I observed Mrs. Kelly preparing a bountiful meal for eight men who had come to help Mr. Kelly with the threshing.   Never have I seen nor smelled such a wonderful array of food.   I remember the table and the men who had come to help Mr. Kelly, filling their plates again and again.

No one ever left Mrs. Kelly's dinner table hungry.

As years went by, Mrs. Kelly and I became closer friends. When I graduated from high school near the top of my class, as had her sons and daughters, she invited me to the room where graduation pictures of her children were displayed on an old upright piano.

She was very proud of her family. There was my graduation picture, now displayed next to those of her children. This was Mrs. Kelly's way of showing how much she cared for me.

She was proud of my achievements too, and there couldn't have been any clearer proof.

After high school, I became employed in the town where I'd grown up, although I now lived half an hour's drive away. Driving back and forth each day; arranging to arrive for work a little early so I could spend time visiting with Mrs. Kelly in the County Farm kitchen as she was busily preparing meals for the residents and baking bread for her special customers.

The aroma of those wonderful baking loaves continued to greet me at the door.

A few years later, I married and went to live in a neighboring town.

Opportunities to visit Mrs. Kelly were few. I felt lonely and sad without friends I'd left behind in the town where I'd grown to adulthood.

I often shared my feelings with Mrs. Kelly. She offered me the understanding of a caring friend.

At the birth of our first child, Mrs. Kelly came to the hospital to visit. As I recall, that was the only occasion on which I saw her away from her home at the County Farm.

Putting her hand on my arm as she stood near my bed, she said; "Now you'll never be lonely again". I needed to hear that.

Time passed.

One day, while visiting in my former town, I decided to go and spend some time with Mrs. Kelly at the farm. She wasn't home. I was told she was in the hospital.

Going directly to the hospital, I sat down in the waiting room. Just then, Mr. Kelly came through the inner door.

He was crying.

I was informed by a nurse that Mrs. Kelly had suddenly gone into cardiac arrest...and died.

Our times together had ended, but as you can see, treasured memories have remained.

"Where your treasure is, there will your heart be also."

* * * *

One Sunday, as I sat in church next to my sister, I noticed she was holding the hymnal in such a way that all I could see was the end of her thumb. It was gripping the hymnal at the bottom of the book, and I began to laugh. Perhaps it was more than a laugh, more like a chuckle, which turned into laughter. She wasn't happy with me, but it was okay because I was so happy with the sight of her thumb were it shouldn't be resting; there was enough laughter for both of us.
As I recall, my parents weren't too happy with their giggling daughters; they were seated in the pew directly behind us.
(I already mentioned to you that I remember unusual incidents; this was one of them.)

My hometown was a pleasant place and it remains so to this day, the way I remember it; the people who live there now have done their very best to retain the look of the town as it was in years gone by.
. From Kindergarten thru the eleventh grade I was privileged to attend the same school in town.
I loved school.

When I was seventeen, my family moved to a neighboring town and the sadness of realizing I wasn't going to be able to graduate from the school I loved with the friends I'd always known, was overwhelming.

I must have convinced my parents of my feelings during the summer months because they decided to let me travel the thirty miles each day to attend school in my home town for my senior year.
In order to do that, my Mother (who was a nurse) acquired a job in a doctor's office and together she and I drove the distance each day so I would be able to attend

school.

In later years I learned my parents were required to pay tuition for me to continue attending the distant school. The amount was $200. Doesn't seem like much now, but comparing the value of currency in 1953 to its value now, two hundred dollars would have been worth around $1500. Two hundred dollars was a significant amount in those years.

After graduation in 1953, I acquired a position as bookkeeper for a small business in my former home town and remained employed there until my marriage in 1955.
* * * *
In 1952, my sister Thelma, who was five years older, married Larry, and soon began her family.

Her husband's brother, Don, was in the service at the time, and although I knew his name, I'd never met him. I do remember him coming to the house one day to pick up Larry's car which was at our house because Larry was there visiting my sister. As I peaked around the kitchen door into the living room, I could see "him" standing at the door waiting for Larry to come and give him the keys to the car. I remember Don was wearing a yellow scarf around his neck.... I finally met him face to face in 1954, We began to date.

Don and I married in 1955.

Sisters were now married to brothers. You could say my sister became my sister-in-law and the children we would eventually have were double-cousins; creating close family ties in the years to come.

With both sets of grandparents living in the same town, it was a perfect setup for the grand-kids.
* * * *
Don and I purchased a home on Houghton Lake, just before we were married in 1955. We bought it furnished; it was fairly new, about three years old.

In 1959 we purchased an old 20 acre farm and moved our family, including two little boys 3 years and 6 months of age, from the lakefront home we had purchased before our marriage.

Life At Hidden Meadows Farm

Married four years in 1959, living on the lakeshore
with a toddler of three and an infant of six months,
we began to look for another, safer, and perhaps more friendly place to live.

Safer? That was my way of thinking.

I've never learned to swim. And we were living on the lakefront,
surrounded on three sides by water.
In addition to the lake at the front, there were deep canals to the north and west.

Now what?

We had no preconceived idea regarding the style of home for which we were
searching.
Looking at several locations, none seemed to provide the answer.

Someone told us there was an old farm for sale nearby.
Perhaps we should look into that possibility.

Neither of us had been raised on a farm. So, the idea of buying a farm was a bit of a
stretch.

Approaching the owners, we learned the farm included twenty acres,
a cobblestone house and an old barn. A local business had planted pine trees to
later harvest for Christmas trees at both ends of the long and narrow property.

Checking it out, we found there was also an old garage, a chicken coop, root cellar
and corn crib.

We decided to take a look.

The old farmhouse had been built by the sons of the original owners in 1936.
We've always assumed that's when it was constructed
since the date is embedded at the top of the 13 cement steps leading to the
basement.
Eventually we learned the barn had been built in 1917.
It was in need of painting along with other repairs
about which we hadn't yet learned.

After our visit with the owners, we talked on our way home.
"Well, what do you think?" my husband asked.
"I liked it", I said. *"And you know what, I felt like I'd been there before"*.
He responded, *"So did I"*.

It seemed this was where we were meant to be.

In 2023 our family is celebrating our 64th year of   living at

Hidden Meadows Farm.

(A name I gave it because there is an 8 acre hayfield which cannot be seen from the house; a "hidden meadow".)

My husband and I were in retail businesses.
Don owned and operated an Ace Hardware and Sporting Goods for 33 years while I eventually owned and operated a Hallmark Shop for 14 years.

During those years of involvement in retail businesses, we also raised sheep for ten years.

A flock of 100 was ours
when we sold them in 1998.   At that time, since we both had retired from retail, we purchased a fifth-wheel and made plans to look around this great country in which we live.

Over the years, we've had goats, pigs and chickens. Our pasture afforded us the opportunity to have horses
for our sons and grandchildren.
We've also entertained ducks and geese and peacocks.

(Or did they entertain us?)

For twenty five years we boarded horses; loved looking out the window and seeing horses in the pasture.

Many wonderful dogs have graced our acreage,
including a St. Bernard , German Shepherd, and a Collie.   Several hunting dogs added greatly to the enjoyment of our sons.
Last but not least, we enjoy the one we have now, a Toy Poodle.
Yes, there were a few cats too.

(I seem to remember a rabbit living in the house for a time. But, that's another story.)

When we first arrived, there was an apple orchard
which has now been reduced to four trees.

(They have grown old even though we have not.)

We have two pear trees
still producing very, very small fruit.
This year, one tree produced two pears.

(*It may be time to plant new trees.*)
In the beginning of life on Hidden Meadows Farm, we had a small orchard of
cherry trees.

There are enough maple trees surrounding the house and barn to hang ten or
twelve sap buckets in early spring.
Many labor intensive hours have provided us
with wonderful maple syrup for the family.

Those hours of labor were, of course, provided by my husband.

The years of "Living The Life" which have been given to our family
at this wonderful homestead are indeed a treasure.

When we were considering the purchase many years ago,
we asked my Dad, who was a carpenter by trade in his early years,
what he thought about the place.

He said, *"There's probably nothing that's level or evenly matched.
It seems solid enough, though.
If I were you I wouldn't put much money in it,
because you don't know how long you'll be living here."*

If he could only have known!

* * * *

I was twenty and Don was twenty-five when we married in 1955. We became
parents for the first time in 1956..a son..Donald Craig. In 1958 we welcomed our
second son, Tim. In 1962, three years after moving to the farm, our third son,
Christopher was born.

When Chris was about two, (that would mean I was twenty-nine), a lovely lady from
the Methodist Church called me from time to time, inviting us to attend church.
She had been teaching in that little church for many years and in fact, had taught
my husband when he was 10 years of age when it was a Community Church. Now it
was part of the Methodist denomination. Her approach was pleasant and the first
thing she would say was, *"And how are those dear little boys of yours"*. Then she
would offer the invitation and the conversation was soon over.

Undoubtedly because of her gentle urgings, one day, I decided to take my boys to
church and that was the beginning for me.

Our two older boys were baptized and confirmed in the church when they reached
the age of twelve; as I had been in my home town when I was twelve.
The plan, of course, was to wait until Chris (our youngest) was twelve, and have
him baptized and confirmed also.

*(In the United Methodist Church, baptism can be done at any age. If your choice is infant
baptism, youth, or adult it may be accomplished at your request)*

One day, I read something in the church commentaries that caught my attention. It
was a description of baptism, saying it was like a keyhole in a door. The only way
you could enter was to have the key. The *key* was baptism.
We arranged for our youngest son to be baptized as soon as the church schedule
could accommodate it.

The instant I understood the message, the responsibility was on us.
Don't wait, do it now.

I attended church every Sunday. Being the strong minded person I am (yes, I
admit it), I had decided not to take Holy Communion just yet. I felt, right or
wrong, I shouldn't be taking it until I had decided to accept Christ. Not sure that I
had seriously made that decision, I would sit quietly as the congregation went
forward for communion. The first opportunity I had to participate after I had
decided to accept, I sat quietly in the pew awaiting the invitation to go forward.
While I was in prayer, the usher (a lovely gentleman from the congregation) kept
talking to me as I quietly waited for my turn. My first "planned" communion
passed me by. (I made it next time though; I've never forgotten that somewhat
funny, but pleasant, visit I had with the usher on Sunday morning.)
(God has a sense of humor I guess. It was to be His timing and not mine.)

I still don't believe in coincidence.

Singing in the high-school glee club, as it was called at that time, was fun for me. As
I recall I sang low alto.
When I began to attend church in my late twenties, I joined the choir. My voice is
what you might call "pleasant". That's about it!. However I was given the
opportunity to sing a solo on occasion and enjoyed doing it.
When a song called "He Touched Me"came out, it was well received by the
Christian community and beautiful. I wanted to sing it, but not yet. I felt as though
He hadn't "touched me" and singing it would not seem truthful to me. So I didn't

sing it.

Coincidence?

During the early seventies, I was dealing with strong feelings against a member of the congregation who often led the service until the pastor arrived from the first two of his 3-point charge. (Serving 3 churches every Sunday.)
One day, I decided to talk with the minister about my difficult feelings. I went to the church on a week-day afternoon and asked to talk to him. I told him my feelings about the man who I knew to be dis-honest. I couldn't accept his leadership of the Sunday worship knowing of his character. It caused me actual pain in my heart to listen to him on Sunday morning at the beginning of the service; leading us in prayer.

The minister said, "Let's pray about it".
So we walked to the front of the church and each of us knelt at the communion rail. He prayed. In his prayer he asked God to give "me" love for the gentleman in question.

I couldn't believe my ears. He was asking for "me" to be given "love" for the offender. I didn't come here for that. I wanted this fellow out of the way. But, the prayer was over and I went on my way wondering if the minister knew what he was doing, or maybe he just didn't understand my situation.

Guess what happened. I learned to love this person in Christian love. He sang in the choir which I led for over twenty-nine years.
He didn't change.
I did.
He passed away several years ago as a good and long time friend of mine, and I treasure the friendship we had.

No coincidence there. Or is there?

Leading the church choir for almost thirty years was the joy of my life. Or, should I say, "*one of the joys?*"

It was a position of leadership I never thought I'd have.

The opportunity to lead a choir, was a miracle in itself. No music background for me, unless you count the fact that I played the cello in the high school orchestra for four years.

I suppose that would count as music training.

Then, I bought a used guitar and learned to play 3 changes. And, there was the accordion which allowed me to pick out a few tunes by ear.

(I do have what some refer to as "a good ear".)

In the early seventies, I joined our church choir. Not long after I joined, the director retired from the position of leadership. Then there was a job opening, not a paying job, a job of service.

(This is key..a job of service.)

Two or three people turned down the position which had opened up. Someone said to me, *"why don't you take it?"* (Obviously, they wanted someone who could wave their hand and tap their foot in time with the music.)

Apparently, I looked as though I could do that.

Honesty is often the best policy.

My response to the invitation was, *"I don't think I'm qualified for the job."* One of the choir members said, *"I don't think you are either."*

But, another lady, who happened to be a trained soloist, a music major, and the music teacher in our local school system, said, *"I think you can do it. Why don't you give it a try?"*

(A note here..)

If you find yourself hesitating about your ability to accept a responsibility, and a person you know who is qualified in the area in question, says you can do it.. do it!)

Continuing..

I loved it!

Years passed and the happiness I felt in the arena of music continued. My musical knowledge improved as the years went by.

The songs I chose for the choir filled my heart with joy. If I didn't feel the joy, I didn't choose that particular piece of music. And, that's an important part of my story.

One or two of my choir members suggested that we sing some "higher church" music or "more classical" music. I said, "*No. I don't care for that style of music.*"

Time went on.

And one evening a meeting was held for the musicians of the church, including the organist, the pianist, the minister of the church and any choir members who wished to attend, and me.

The subject of choir music choices was introduced by someone, maybe me. The minister said to me, "*What would you like to do about introducing different kinds of music?*"

I responded, "*If that's what you want, you can get yourself another choir director.*"

Instantly...A voice in my mind, (the voice I heard was a male's voice), and it said:

"*Who do you serve?*"

I was astonished! I dropped my head to rest on my arms on the table before me. A moment passed. *(See note at end of article.)*

I raised my head, looked at the minister, and said, "*I'll do whatever it is you want me to do.*"

The conversation immediately took on a different tone; pleasant, agreeable, "*no big deal*" they said. And continued, "*just once in awhile when you run across something different, take a look at it.*"

And the meeting soon adjourned.

What do you suppose was the chance I would have come up with such a response on my own? I had been determined to have it my way.

"*Who do you serve*"; the voice said. (It was a voice, not a thought.)

To be honest with you, I was serving myself. It was all about me at that stage of my service.

You'll need to believe me when I tell you it was a male voice I heard in my mind. It was very clear, short, and to the point.

14

"Who do you serve?"

Today, more than 40 years have passed since this incident. It has remained a very clear memory. It has never happened again.

Who do you serve?

I serve Him!
(Note: When the meeting had finished, I told the lady sitting next to me, (a pianist from our church whose name was Shirley), what had happened to me; the voice, the question.. She said, "I wondered what had happened when you dropped your head down so quickly to the table in front of you.")

(Did I mention that I don't believe in coincidence?)

Actively attending services every Sunday, when the boys were young I usually took them with me. But as time went on, the boys were older and not interested in Sunday morning church. My husband owned and operated a retail business in our small town resort area, and worked on Sundays, leaving me to attend church by myself; leading the choir each Sunday morning.

There was opportunity for me not only to attend, but to teach Sunday school classes for many different ages from elementary to high school to adult. Reaching into the depths of my understanding and gaining knowledge of Christ has always been a part of my search.

Through the seventies I worked alongside my husband in his place of business while maintaining the family and the home.

In the early months of 1977, several of our church members became concerned that we weren't growing in Christ as we wanted to be, and we came together to discuss it. We decided to meet each Sunday after church, in the kitchen,coming together and praying for our congregation to reach out to Christ. As many as thirty came at first, and prayed together for twenty minutes. Each person could offer a prayer, or not, as they wished. As the weeks went by the attendance diminished and eventually we decided to end our gathering times.
No answers to our prayers seemed evident.

In early fall of that same year, our church decided to hold seminars which were entitled, "Life In The Spirit". Always interested in more understanding of the Christian walk, I attended them, as did many.

The central theme of the seminars was the "gifts of the Spirit", among them "the gift of tongues". This was an area with which I was unfamiliar. I was interested in the happening as mentioned in scripture at the time of Pentecost. At our seminar, many went forward asking for the Gift and were receiving it in prayer. As I observed it seemed to be real. But I decided if it was real, then I didn't have to receive the "gift" at the church building, at the appointed meeting time.
So I didn't ask. I didn't receive.
I explained to our minister my feelings about the subject.
He *said, "that's fine, if you receive the gift at any time in the future, let me know."*

Never having read the Bible from Genesis to Revelation, I've always been one to search for areas of interest to find answers to my questions. I have never memorized chapter and verse but the index usually leads me to answers.

One morning in November of 1977, as I was vacuuming the carpet in the living room in my housecoat and slippers, I decided to pray to receive the "gift of tongues".

But before I go further, I should tell you I had always had a fear of death. That fear had been with me all my life. Sometimes I would wake up in the night in a panic. Turning on the light to calm myself, I would try to get the fear off my mind and go back to sleep. *(Back to my story.)*

The instant I asked for the gift of tongues, I received. The unfamiliar sounds came seemingly unbidden from my voice and I knew my request had been fulfilled.

Just as quickly came this in my thoughts; *"In my Father's house are many mansions. If it were not so, I would have told you. I go to prepare a place for you. Where I am you may be also."*

I cried.
As soon as I could gain control of my emotions, I called the minister and told him I had received the gift. And told him, also, of the revelation.
I didn't know where it was in scripture at that moment. The minister told me it was John 14. I had received the knowledge of scripture I hadn't known existed. It appeared in my heart and mind.

I have never experienced the fear of death again.

Did I tell you I don't believe in coincidences?

Eventually, a thought invaded my mind. We had prayed for God to move our church in some way during the early months of the same year at the seminars. We didn't feel He'd answered our prayers at that time.
You might say we gave up.
He didn't.

I'm sure He already knew the date and the time and exactly who He would call to attend the fall meetings. Our church began to move forward in an observable way.

There's that "coincidence" thing again.
I still don't believe in them.

* * * *

Remembering Ann

A gift to   cherish....

Ann lived a short distance from our house.
She and her husband moved to the neighborhood
from the southern part of the state
where she had worked in a factory and he had been employed
as a heavy equipment operator.

Now retired, they spent their time caring for their home.

Having no children, they were deeply devoted to each other.

Plain looking and soft spoken,
Ann had the proverbial heart of gold.
Her graying hair was not stylishly fixed
in the fashion of the day.

Each year she raised a beautiful circular flower garden
highlighting a birdbath in the center.

It was surrounded by colorful flowers.

The garden prospered under Ann's tender care.

She and her husband were always nearby,   lending a helping hand
when one was needed.

Appearing on a summer's evening to visit for a time,
there was always encouragement for us in planning our young lives,
with an offer to help in any way they could.

Ann unwittingly helped me to acquire a taste for sauerkraut.
I could never abide the bitter taste no matter how I tried.
One day, I stopped by her house.
The wonderful aroma in her kitchen caused me to inquire
about what she was cooking.

Her answer was, sauerkraut.
I shared with her my utter dislike for it.
Ann suggested I should add brown sugar
and a couple of quartered apples to the sauerkraut as it cooked.

What a difference that combination made.

Perhaps there's a lesson here.
It may be the lack of seasoning in our lives that causes bitterness.
The addition of something sweet,
can change bitterness to joy
and gives us a new appetite for life.

One day, I was told Ann was in the hospital for stomach surgery.
The results were not good.
She had cancer and nothing could be done.

Ann came home to spend her remaining days
in her own bed, in her own home,

surrounded by things and people she loved.

By then, Ann was in her late sixties.

Life for me, at that time,
had been completely turned around
by the joy and knowledge of the Holy Spirit.

The Bible was exciting.

Scripture was leaping off the pages of the Bible, to me,
as it had never done before.

I prayed incessantly for Ann's healing.
My faith was strong and each day I prayed for more. I was asking for complete
healing of Ann's body.

Time passed and healing for my friend was not evident.

I searched scripture for more information.
There were many passages for guidance.
(1Thess.5:27 *"pray without ceasing".)*

The disciples asked Jesus
why they had not had a healing for someone
by praying for them.
Jesus responded; (Matthew 17:21)
*"this kind does not go out
except by prayer and fasting."*
Further (in Mark) it is noted He said to them.,
"This kind can come out by "nothing" but prayer and fasting".

For the first and only time in my life, I fasted.

I prayed without ceasing for 24 hours.

The fasting directed my complete attention to the prayer,
to Ann, and
to the Holy Spirit.

I was confident that Ann would be healed.

She was not healed.

A few weeks later, Ann died.

I questioned God, my faith, and myself.

Ann was a devout Catholic, and
her funeral was held in our local Catholic Church.

My family sat in the back of the church
quietly observing the unfamiliar (to us) funeral rituals.

I was sad for the loss of my friend, Ann.

The words of the service fell on closed ears and a heavy heart.

Suddenly I was amazed.

A great feeling of joy began to well up within me.
I felt overwhelmed with the knowledge being given to me, in my mind and heart.

Ann was healed.
She was in heaven.

The promises of God were fulfilled.
"I go to prepare a place for you. Where I am you will be also."

The Holy Spirit was giving to me the knowledge of her healing.

I received the confirmation of her new life
as a gift from God.

It is a gift I will remember and cherish all the days of my life.

It truly is a gift to be shared.

One treasures the people in life who made a difference

in the way we lived then,

and now.

I would not have identified Ann as such an important person,
until my experience at the time of her death.

I now believe that God called me to Ann's friendship
so He could show me

His Way.

It's hard to explain my experience the day of Ann's funeral.

The feeling was instant, intense and oh so joyful.

I've shared the experience
with friends and family.
There is no way to convey
the intensity of the joy I felt
as I sat quietly in the back row of an unfamiliar church
during an equally unfamiliar funeral service.

Maybe that was part of God's plan too.

Belief in Ann's healing
and belief in life after life,
in a perfect state of being
will never change for me.

It truly is

A GIFT TO BE SHARED

****

I still don't believe in coincidence.

Thinking about dreams, one day, it came to mind how often I had encountered a
repeated dream in my life. That's called a "reoccurring dream", or so they tell me.

It was always the same. I was walking through a familiar hallway, and passed an open door that led to a stairway. Finding myself at the top of the stairs, there was another hallway. On either side of the hallway, as I walked by, were empty rooms.

That's it; end of dream. After my gift of the holy spirit and my newfound, strengthened belief in God, I never had the dream again.

I began to wonder about it.

Although I'm not much for interpreting dreams, which I rarely have, I decided that the dream was symbolic of my inner search for Christ.

The rooms at the top of the stairs were empty. They had represented my search for fulfillment. Once they were filled, the dream disappeared.

I must say I still don't believe in "coincidence". However, there are additional observations in my life; God's presence, my observance of His presence, His gifts, and my service.

There may be more to come.

I hope so.

A new idea recently crossed my mind; *the future is today.*

I need to give that some serious thought.

FAMILY
MOMENTS

Alive And In Step
The Rescue
Finding The Thread
Where There Is Sadness, Joy

Alive And In Step

Walking is good for me.
It's good for my soul; a clear mind, ears hearing the song of the
smallest bird; legs which strengthen as I increase the distance.

Wildlife hides from me.
Though often seen in the neighborhood through which I walk,
they quickly hide from my approaching footsteps.

Little birds, hidden among the leaves in the tallest trees, send
songs to me as I walk by.

My mind is active; pondering unsolved problems and
remembering bits of conversations of the past.
Snippets of once learned lyrics skip through my thoughts.

I feel alive and in step with the Spirit.

My Prayer:
Lord, let me walk with you every day, along life's way.

Galatians 5:25
"Since we live by the Spirit, let us keep in step with the Spirit "(NIV)

The Rescue

"Night fell, darkness hid the two from sight"

He worked at walking.

Stumbling,

weaving,

tumbling,

falling...

Each night at dusk he turned for home, deaf to traffic sounds. Reeling into roadside ditch, he lay upon the ground in bleak half-conscious stupor.

With effort, he crawled to the ditch's edge,

then worked at walking

once again.

The man continued through his nightly ritual.

My friend approached the sodden hulk. Bending down, he knelt beside the fallen man; with strong and steady arms, he began *"The Rescue"*....

My friend was not a hero; I was only an observer. Though years have passed, the vivid scene remains.

Whose life was changed? Whose journey reached a crossroad? Whose path was interrupted by a chance encounter?

Was it the man? Was it my friend? Was it me?

What are *you* thinking now?

Night fell. Darkness hid the two from sight.

"The Rescue" had begun.

copyright@2020

It has been many years since this incident took place.

My husband and I were standing at our living room window, watching a man walking down the distant road.

He lived nearby in a broken down house. Every day he walked two miles to a neighborhood bar where he spent the long hours of the day.

We didn't always see him traveling on the way to his daily destination. Nor did we see him when he was going home at day's end.

But this day, we saw him walking toward his home.

He staggered and stumbled, repeatedly falling into the deep ditch

beside the road.

For moments he was out of our sight. Then, once more, we saw him crawling up the side of the ditch and struggling to his feet. Walking a few steps, he fell once more. Again he crawled to the top of the ditch on his hands and knees and attempted to stand.

I became aware my husband was no longer standing by my side.

Now, in his truck, he was driving down our driveway toward the distant road. Stopping at the place where the man was lying beside the ditch, my husband got out of his truck and approached the figure.

Taking him by the arm, he helped the man to his feet.

My husband later told me he had intended to help the man into the cab of the truck, but the man protested. *"I'm not clean enough to sit in your truck. Help me into the back. I'll ride home there."*

As this scene unfolded before my eyes, I was surely not aware it would remain in my memory and my heart, these many years later.

How many of us, including me, would leave the comfort of home to help an obviously drunken man get safely to his home?

This was a side of my husband about which I wasn't aware at the time. Yes, he was kind, gentle and caring. The scene I watched was more than that.

The experience changed me. Maybe it has changed you.

At this stage of life it has become clear to me, we all need to be rescued.

Our *Friend* is on *His* way.

As time passed, we discussed the incident; facts revealed themselves about the man who was rescued.

He was a veteran from World War 2.

We have since become aware of the experiences our soldiers endured during that time which were too horrible for them to remember.

We now call it PTSD.

It has been found, for some of the veterans, it is easier to drink away the memories than to relive them in their minds.

In our village, there were three World War 2 veterans who spent their days at the same local bar.

The world called them drunks. Should we have called them heroes?

How do you feel about it?

Finding The Thread

The thread begins to reveal itself. Ahead are endless, unplanned days.

This wasn't supposed to happen to me.

"We have to have a plan," I told everyone. But where was *my* plan? If I could see ahead, just a little, maybe I could unravel the thread.

Walking into our spare bedroom this morning, the view turned from dark to sunshine.

A scene exploded in my memory.

I could see my father lying on the bed we borrowed from Hospice. We wanted his last days to be spent with a view of our peaceful world; the trees, the horses in the pasture.

I hope he loved the quiet scenes before him.

"The Lord is my Shepherd...

He makes me to lie down in green pastures.   He restores my soul"

I hope my Dad's soul was restored.

He knew what he was facing. He wouldn't talk to us about it; that was his way of dealing with the impending transition.

(A visiting minister later revealed that Dad had asked him what heaven was like. I think we all may have that question in our hearts.)

We visited with Dad as often as we could, as did many friends in those last few days.

We could only face the situation by continuing our daily routines. Dad did his best to honor our game.

He didn't retire until the age of sixty-nine. It seemed like a grand old age to me, in those years, but now it seems rather young.

He always had a plan, a routine, an interest, and a goal. He was disciplined, determined, loving and reliable, committed to his family.

What about me?

I have many questions; not many answers. I want my life to count for something. Have I stopped counting?

What happens in a single parent family when the parental balance does not exist?

What happens to the marriage, with no plans for commitment?

 The last two generations have given us a preview of a very different society.

Has the media become the parent? Is the media making our moral judgments?

"Everyone is doing it, and I want to do it too."

Blame for bad outcomes can always be affixed to someone, somewhere, somehow.

By what moral standards does this new generation make its' decisions?

There is a new intensity in my nightly prayers.

He is much closer.

My time to see Him face to face is much nearer than before.

Mary Anne Whitchurch Tuck

Where There Is Sadness, Joy

Always Generous, Gracious and Giving

Mother was my joy.   Now she's gone.

I asked her, a few hours after Grandma died;
"How does it make you feel?"
"Like an orphan", was her answer.
"But Mother", I responded, *"You have us."*
"I know honey", she said. *"But this is different."*

Carrying our second child,
I was filled with the joy of life; annoyed at having to deal with
death.
I wanted Mother to tell me it wasn't so bad.
Grandma was old. Eighty years was a long full life.
In a coma, Grandma hadn't suffered.

I wanted Mother to move on to lighter talk and future plans.
I wanted her to ask how I was feeling today,
resuming our daily ritual.

She was always the giver. I was always the taker.

Years passed and now Mother was in her eighties.
She shared with me the ominous news;
she had found a lump in her breast.
"Mother" I said, *"I am absolutely sure it will not be malignant."*

When the report came back, Mother said,
*"Well, you were wrong. It is malignant and the involvement is
extensive".*

Now, I who never wanted to deal with anything uncomfortable,
was required to face the unimaginable.
Mother was going to die.
Try as I would, I couldn't get my mind around that fact.

A friend said to me,
"It's part of life, although it's not the best part."

I was angry with my friend
for her crude and thoughtless remark.
How could she be so matter of fact in the face of my
devastation?

My friend offered.   I refused.

In the days and months to follow,
Mother calmly accepted the diagnosis;
always generous, always caring, always gracious and giving.

She was ever accepting. I was ever refusing.

The following January,
my friend and I vacationed for two weeks in Florida.
Upon our return I learned that Mother had suffered a heart attack
a few days earlier.
She didn't want me to be told about it
because she wanted me to enjoy my vacation.
I could learn of it when I returned home.

She was always protecting.   I was always accepting.

I visited Mother in the hospital the day after returning home from
my vacation. As she lay in her bed she was cheerful
and as usual, interested in me.

"Maybe it wasn't so serious after all", I said.
She answered *"No, something very serious is going on."*
She began to talk to me of times of joy; speaking of happy things
and times and places.

As I left her on Saturday, I said,
"See you when you come home".
"Ok honey", she said,

for she was due to come home on Monday.
She would be in the hospital one more day.

Early Monday morning, while still in the hospital, we were
notified Mother had died.

Mother always gave me her love. I always accepted it.

She was gone.
I felt smothered by a blanket of grief.
Mother was as much a part of my life as my heart and soul.
Now she was gone.
Her belongings were still here; her clothes hung in the closet.
Pictures she had painted hung on the wall.
They were only "things".

Weeks passed and my seemingly endless river of tears
began to subside.

On a stark February night, I visited my friend who lives in the
country and is a shepherd.

It was lambing time,
and she made frequent visits to the barn
checking on the well being of the ewes.

I found her there
and we began to talk.
Surrounded by the rumblings of her flock
and the sweet smell of freshly scattered straw,
the rawness of my grief began to pour out.

With gentle encouragement
my friend shared her own journey
through the painful loss of both parents
during the preceding years.

With deep compassion she shared her healed grief.
I knew that with her consoling love,
I too would be healed through this journey of grieving.

My friend offered. I accepted.

Next morning as I prepared the morning coffee,
my glance fell upon a plaque hanging on the kitchen wall.
Reading it as if for the first time,
I understood the message of St. Francis of Assisi.

Lord, make me an instrument of thy peace;
Where there is hatred, let me sow love;
Where there is injury, pardon;
Where there is doubt, faith;
Where there is despair, hope;
Where there is darkness, light;
And where there is sadness, joy.

Divine Master, grant that I may not so much seek to be consoled
as to console;
to be understood as to understand;
to be loved as to love;
for it is in the giving that we receive,

it is in pardoning that we are pardoned,
and it is in dying that we are born to eternal life.

Dear Lord
Thank you for the loving, giving people you have placed in my life.
Help me to be the consoling, understanding, loving and giving instrument of
your peace
which has so graciously been given to me.

Amen

A LITTLE HUMOR NEVER HURTS

Life Changing Events
Guess Who Ran The Red Light
When You Come To A Fork In The Road..Take It
Tell It Like It Was

Life Changing Events

Like the words to an old song, these words keep going around in my mind.

"Nylons Security".

One of my life changing events was in early spring, as I recall.

A few years before, my husband and I had decided to raise sheep.
it happened like this; as it remains in memory.

One day, I suggested we should get a lamb.
After all, we have this little farm.
Our grandchildren live next door,
it would be fun.

It wasn't long
before my husband came home
announcing
he'd found a lamb.
In fact, he'd found two, a male and a female.
They were orphans.
They needed people to love and care for them.

That would be us.

I don't remember the exact time frame
as events began to unfold, but it wasn't long after the arrival of the orphan lambs
that I casually suggested we should start a flock, you know, become shepherds.

"We already have "Bo" and "Betsy" and the grandchildren love them."

We also had this big old barn with nothing in it; as in animals.

It was then we began our search for mature ewes.
We would use them to build our flock.
We had "Bo", but he wasn't what you'd call a breeder yet,

He would be, though, in a year or so
when he was no longer "a lamb." (You get the idea.)

The plan to become shepherds   was quickly put into action.

We were proud and excited about our new farming endeavor.

My husband had been in the retail hardware business for several years.
I owned and operated a Hallmark shop.
This would be fun;
A little something extra to give us a new hobby.

One day a gentleman came to call
who was interested in our lambing operation.
Of course, I was more than happy to show him our nearly 100 year old barn where
our new flock resided.

Now, this is the point where I veer away from the sheep/shepherd situation
and explain some of my personal habits to you.
I wouldn't even be telling you this
if it wasn't that I had recently seen posts on Facebook
from women
who had found themselves involved in the same situation
I experienced
on my journey to the barn that day.

Without getting too personal,   I'm going to reveal my lifetime habit of getting ready
for bed at night; included in my habit,
would be the removing of my jeans and underwear
in one swift motion.
Unfortunately this has, on occasion,
caused a slight "public" embarrassment.
(*How could that be?* I should explain, since I would be
getting ready for bed *"at night, at home."*)

How could that possibly affect my actions in the daytime? Hmm...

Back to the fine gentleman
who had come to look at our flock of sheep.

We were walking toward the barn
when he turned around,
looked quickly back in the direction of the driveway near the house, and said...
"Oh! You've dropped your hanky."

Intuitively, as I turned, I knew what I was about to see.

The clump of white lying in the driveway
was instantly recognizable to me.
It was definitely not my hanky.
It was my underwear,
which had been clinging,
(with the help of static electricity from the dryer,)
to the inside of my jeans.
The undergarment had chosen that moment
to release itself from the fabric of my jeans,
and to embrace the ground
in the driveway.

"I'll get it", he said,
turning around and taking a step
toward the object.
"No", I said,
"I'll get it".
We were immediately in competition
to find out who would get to *"the hanky"*... first .

I outran him by seconds,
scooped up *'the hanky'*
and shoved 'it'
into my jacket pocket.

Bless his heart, he seemed totally unaware of the rapid beating of my heart, which
was not caused from the exertion of running to the area of the driveway in question.

One might think
the *hanky* experience would have been a lesson
forever etched in my mind. It was definitely time to review and perhaps renew, a
few of my habits.

However, that was not to be.

Continuing...

One quiet morning in summer
I had personally opened my Hallmark Shop at nine a.m.
so my employees wouldn't have to come in

until later.

A pleasant fellow was the first to stop by.
He stood just inside the front door,
where we visited for twenty minutes or so.

As he turned to leave, he said,
*"You may want to check the leg of your slacks
near your shoe"*.

With that, he went upon his way.

Looking down at my shoe,
in full view,
was a visible display of one of my knee-high nylons,
which was making its way
past the static electricity in my slacks to heaven knows where.

Can you imagine
what the nice fellow must have been thinking
as we stood there and talked?
He apparently had decided
he would share his observation with me as our conversation ended
and he went out the door. As I recall, he didn't look back.

I don't know if men are prone to giggling.
But I'll bet this fellow was giggling as he made the way to his car.

At this moment,
it's important for me to tell you
I've never had either of these experiences again.

I really have changed my habits;
about *certain* things.

Although my friends and family would tell you that it is rare for me to change my
mind, I still have some *habit* changing to do.

For Christmas that year,
my family gave
me a bottle of fabric softener
and a pair of nylons

with lace edged suspenders attached to them.

One of the habit changes I have yet to make
is to not to share with anyone
the embarrassing things that happen to me.
I'm not sure if one could call them "life-changing" events, but
I really do need to change my ways!
(Some of them.)

Guess Who Ran The Red Light
For the record, it wasn't me.

I've always bragged about my driving record.
As with many, I started driving at the age of 16.

Granted, I've never traveled much cross-country
or in a foreign land, (such as Canada).
Still, no person of the law enforcement
has ever flagged me down on the highway.

I've always been quite proud of that.

Oh yes, there was that time in New Hampshire.
Returning to the campground where our fifth-wheel waited;
my husband was tired so I was driving.

It was almost midnight.
You may wonder why the time would be of importance.
There were no cars to be seen on the road through town;

(Manchester, New Hampshire.)

Trying to navigate the unfamiliar left hand turn at a cross section,
I didn't see the traffic light.
It was blinking red, apparently.

However, the red flashing light of the police car
in the rear-view mirror immediately caught my attention.
The traffic officer appeared at my window.
Why he was cruising this deserted road at mid-night,
I'll never know.
"I didn't see the light, officer", I said.
"I was searching for the turn and guess I was preoccupied".

He was very nice and quietly said,
"You'll need to be more careful in the future".

There was no ticket...whew!

Now let me think.
The only time I received a traffic ticket
was in 2013
when
I was traveling a nearby local highway,
apparently at the speed of 74 mph
in a
55 mph zone.

A township officer, who was hiding in a nearby forest,
must have believed she had a live one,
and followed me persistently
until I pulled to the side of the road.

Informing me she had clocked my car at 74 mph in a 55 mph zone,
she said *"Don't you have a cruise control?"*
"Yes officer" I said, *"but it doesn't work".*

"I'll have to write you a ticket", she said.
Standing by the car she began to fill out the citation.

"I have not had a ticket since I started to drive at the age of 16,"
I said, smiling quietly." *I suppose I will have to quit telling my friends
I'm a "virgin driver".*
(I was quite sure she'd noticed my birth year of 1935
on the driver's license.)

An understanding smile crossed her face; I've never figured out what it
was that she was *"understanding"*, maybe it was something I said.
"I'll just write the ticket for 60 mph.", she said.
*"But be careful you don't get another within the next three years
or your insurance will increase."*

Thanking her profusely, I drove on my merry way,
silently cherishing my sense of humor
which I inherited from my Mother.

* * *

Continuing:

Last Monday I drove a few miles down the road to our local McDonalds
to buy myself a Big Mac and an order of fries. Just as I left home, my son
said *"Pick me up a large strawberry shake"*.

I did.

As I recall,
the Big Mac and fries
have never been seen again but that's another story.

As is my usual routine, I drove through the Wal-Mart parking lot in
order to re-enter the main road at the stop light. It's much safer.

The light turned green and I moved forward.

In the flash of a moment, I found myself across the main highway and
on the far side of the road; about the same time I heard a loud sound
very close to my driver-side window and felt something hit my left arm
rather harshly. (It turned out to be the air-bag.)

A nice gentleman appeared at my car window
and asked me if I was all right.
"Yes, I'm fine", I said.
(Later was when I found the scrapes and bruises and aches,
but I digress.)

A glance toward the dashboard on the passenger side revealed my
glasses, which I had been wearing. Now, that's interesting. Wonder how
they got over there?

My son came to give me a ride home
and the wrecker took my car away. (I think I gave someone my home
phone number to call and that's how my son knew where to find me;
sitting in the middle of the highway in a crumbled car, still wondering
how my glasses got over there.)

A few days later the insurance adjuster called to inform me
the car was totaled. (Well *duh,* that wasn't hard to see.)

I now have a new car,
a new appreciation for driver side airbags,
an understanding of the need for seat belts which I fortunately had on,
and some other things I haven't thought of yet.
(I still don't know how my glasses got on the passenger side of the car.)
There is also one more thing I've learned. I'd like to share it with you.

You can't always depend on the person who has the red-light at an
intersection
to stop.
It should become a habit to look both ways, and look again, even when
you have the green-light.

"When You Come To A Fork In The Road, Take It!"

(Yogi Berra had the right idea.)

I love to reminisce and write about bygone times, remembering the people I've known, especially those who have made a difference in the *me* I've become at the age of 86. I once thought 86 was really, really old.

It isn't.

Actually, I once believed that 50 was old. As I recall, 50 *was* old when my grandmothers were alive.

I was devastated the day I turned thirty. Life was over, I was no longer "twenty-something". Looking forward, there was nothing left to life.

Ahead were only dreary, boring days and years of waiting to get "old." There was nothing new to do nor places to see or roads to travel.

There were no college years for me.

When I am required to check off my level of education on an application, the box to check must be "graduated high-school".

My Dad always commented, *"Some folks attend college and still don't have enough sense to come in out of the rain."*

I feel good about his comment because my high school education helps me to remember to carry my umbrella on a cloudy day.

That reminds me, a week or so ago I purchased a new umbrella. It was very easy to raise, but for the life of me I couldn't figure out how to lower it when I got inside a building.

You'll be happy to know, with a great deal of concentration, I finally figured out how to return it to its original closed position by pushing the little "down" arrow located right underneath the "up" arrow.

Who says a high school education isn't worth much?

One could hardly think of me as a world traveler, but I've learned much about life from the shores of Michigan's largest inland lake.

Married sixty-two years, my husband and I raised three sons. It's difficult to imagine someone as young as I, having sons who are now in their fifties and sixties.

Facts are not always as they seem.

Life is like a dream.

I heard someone make a statement just the other day about *"alternative"* facts.

(Perhaps I should research some of them when describing my attributes.)

Tell It Like It Was

Can't Take It Any More!

I thought "the *cawf*" would stop if I ignored it, but it didn't. How long would the "*cawf*" remain hidden behind the alphabet, before someone speaks up?

Guess I'll have to do it myself. It's driving me crazy.

At first it was only fashions.

I could live with that. Too long, too short, too loose, too tight; who cares? If the image you see in the mirror doesn't disturb *you*, make your own stylish statement.

Then it was the vehicles we drive.

What happened to the classy look of the Oldsmobile in the fifties? You could always define the brand by the look. Somewhere along the line they all began to look alike. I thought that was sad until the *SUV*'s came along and classy became "*cool*".

It wasn't long before the *SUV's* agreed to share the road with the "*Pick-ups*" and the race was on! "*That's ok*," I said to myself, so I bought a pick-up.

Somewhere along the way, I began listening instead of looking. Changes in the language began to catch my ear; not my eye, but my ear.

The first words I noticed were people speaking of a childhood disease. I heard the words mentioned on television and assumed the person had mispronounced. I waited and listened. (w)*hoo–*

ever the persons were; (w)*hoo-ever* the persons are, they're still pronouncing it incorrectly.

The word is...."(w)Hooping cough".

Say it aloud. That's right, say it now!

Did you just say "Wooping cough"?

You've pronounced it wrong.

I'm here to help.

Because it has become so important to me that the name of this particular childhood disease be spoken correctly,

I've taken the time to look up some helpful facts.

The correct pronunciation is; *"hoo-ping cough".*

(say it aloud)

Did you notice anything? For the sake of time, let me point out the *"W" is silent.* Now repeat after me; (w)*hole-some,* (w)*hole,* (w)*hoo-m,*

(w)hoo-so-ever.

Once more: *hoo-ping Cough*

You'll never understand what it means to me to have cleared this confusion for you.

May *The Force* be with you!

OUR COUNTRY

Proud To Be An American
September 11, 2001

A Very Special Day

Proud To Be An American

A VERY SPECIAL DAY

IN SMALL TOWN AMERICA

Standing beside the highway

we awaited the moment when the parade would come into view.

It's an exciting time for folks, young and old,

to celebrate the lives and service which many have given

for our country.

We could hear the high school band playing

several blocks away

as they announced the arrival of the parade.

"God Bless America"

"I'm Proud To Be An American"

The township fire trucks were blowing their sirens

as they drove slowly along the parade route.

The driver in each truck waved happily to the crowds

as they passed by.

People dressed in clown suits walked on either side of the highway,

giving candy to the children

who were enjoying the fun.

Every side road leading to the main highway

had been blocked off by law enforcement

until the parade had passed.

This year, the highway near the library

was our place to watch the parade.

Next to us, a young Mother and her two little girls

waited excitedly for the moment when the American flag and the high school band

would pass directly in front of them.

I could hear the young woman softly advising her daughters

to stand on the curb when the parade was in view.

She told them,

"When the American flag passes by,

stand quietly with your right hand over your heart;

face the flag until it has passed."

(And she showed them, which hand was the right hand,

and where one's heart is located.)

She didn't know I was listening, but I'm pleased that I was.

Through the years,

and especially the last few years,

I've found that certain memories, can bring a lump to my throat.

This was one of those moments.

I'm sad that we may have forgotten our responsibility

to teach the young children

respect for other people,

their traditions and beliefs and our country's flag.

Perhaps we've forgotten the importance of passing these legacies

to the children of future generations.

It isn't written in a book, it isn't found on television and it isn't a requirement in the schools.

It's up to us!

The quiet young Mother and her little girls left a lasting impression on me.

God Bless The USA

September 11, 2001

NEVER FORGET

"I wanted to feel the comfort of shared grief.
The quilters were a blessing to me."

Standing before the television,
getting my last look at the news
before beginning my day;
I couldn't comprehend the scene before me.

A large plane had flown into the World Trade Center in New York City and
completely disappeared.
Smoke and flames were billowing out
at a point six stories down from the top of the building.

The remnants of the plane had not appeared on the other side of the tower.
It didn't make sense.

Was I watching a video or a re-run.
How could this have happened?

I called to my husband who was working outside.
"Come in here and look at this."

While we stood together before the television,
another large plane appeared; flying into the second tower.

Once again the plane did not appear on the other side; causing an explosion of
smoke and fire.

As the day progressed,
one of the towers completely collapsed and disintegrated into the ground,
sending unbelievable amounts of soot and smoke
racing through the narrow streets.

Hundreds were running away
in an effort to escape the terrible scene; many covered with soot.

An event, which I have never viewed,
although I know it was captured by cameras,
shows thousands of people

jumping from the fire in the collapsing buildings
to their deaths on the ground.

I cannot bring myself to look at it.

It was reported that 400 police officers and fire fighters
were killed
while attempting to rescue as many as possible
from the blazing buildings.
These brave men had led many to safety.

They are heroes.
This is America.
Tragedies of such magnitude don't happen here.

As the day wore on,
it was difficult to draw away from the sight
of the events before me on my television.

I felt fear and a heavy sadness
for what was happening in New York.
How could anyone
living in the United States of America
believe this could be possible?

Thousands of people had gone to work that morning,
never to return to their loved ones.
How do we accept such an event
except through fear, confusion and sadness.

Later, as the hours passed,
a report was given that a passenger plane was down;
Flight 93, had crashed and disintegrated
in a field in Pennsylvania.
Forty unbelievably brave passengers attempted to take over the plane.
All were killed as they tried to retrieve control from the terrorists.

We remember them as heroes.

A report was given of a fourth plane
with 184 passengers aboard
which had flown into the Pentagon in Washington D.C..

Many were killed.

The scenes before me could not be denied.
It was reported Fight 93 had been destined
to destroy the White House.
Because of the actions of the passengers
the plane crashed
into an empty field; taking all to their death.

That night, our church which will hold 300 people,
held a prayer meeting.
Every available place was filled.

It was the beginning of a new awareness.
There are people who hate us because we exist.
They hate us so much, they willingly die
in order to kill as many of us in the United States of America
as possible.

I felt a strong need to reach out to people far away;
wanting to feel the comfort of shared grief.
How could that be accomplished?

My recently developed   hobby of quilting
had led me to discover
a program on the Internet
designed for exchanging quilt materials.

Choose a listed name and address,
send twenty-four two-inch pieces of material
in a variety of colors.

The recipient would sew them into a quilt.

I should send my material to them
and they in turn
would send theirs to me.
Along with the material,
the guidelines suggested also sending

a little note about myself,
where I lived
and briefly about my life.

I received fabric and note exchanges from every state in the union,
including one from Israel.
Eventually there were enough squares
to make a full sized quilt,
covering both sides with the material received.

Opening each package
I felt warmly connected to these women
I would never meet.
I felt strengthened
knowing that their hands
had prepared the material,
which I now held in my hands.

The quilters were a blessing to me.

Each message received I've kept in a folder; remembering friends unknown who
now touched my life.

I was sixty-six years of age in 2001.
My life
and thousands of others,
could never be the same again.

We cannot let the evil existing in the world
change us as persons
or as citizens
of the United States of America.

The events of September 11
have been burned into the minds
of those of us who witnessed it.

To many of our youth,
September 11, 2001,
is only a piece of history.
It may be likened to the story of the First World War,

Viet Nam, or the Korean War.
The difference is,
this took place in the United States of America
in the twenty-first century.

It didn't happen
under the leadership of George Washington
or Abraham Lincoln.

It didn't happen
when Theodore Roosevelt or Harry Truman
held the office of president.

It happened
under the administration
of the forty-third president of the United States of America,

George W. Bush.

To President Bush,
in office for less than one year,
fell the responsibility of dealing with a people who hate us.
These are people
who consider our very existence
to be an affront to their god.

It fell to our president
to comfort
many who were frightened and grief stricken.

This isn't the world in which I grew to adulthood.
Could I have imagined
a foreign nation taking the lives of 3000 people
on a fair September morning in New York city?
Would I have believed
I could be a witness
while standing before a television in my home
as it was happening?

The answer is no.

We must NEVER FORGET September 11, 2001.

The memories remain vivid
on September 11, 2021.
Sad memories come quickly.
I WILL NOT FORGET.

MANNERS

Respectfully Yours

RESPECTFULLY YOURS?

It was a different time when I was growing up In the forties and fifties. We didn't have much first-hand information about disrespect, but we knew a lot about *"respect"*.

Start with the flag, you know the one; stars, stripes, red white and blue?

Remember how we stood up when the Star Spangled Banner was played at the football games? No one made us, we just did it. *(Hand over heart and facing the flag.)* Now, some folks are tired of it. Let's drop down on one knee and look toward the ground.

How about *"stand on your own two feet and make a difference"* in honor of something worthwhile?

Remember when you were told to address the friends of your parents by *Mr.* and *Mrs.*? In our home, we were informed a doctor should not be addressed as *"Doc"*.

He was educated to be a doctor. We will show him respect by calling him *"Dr. Jones"*. Our teachers were also spoken of as *Mr. and Mrs, or Miss.* They were never to be referred to as *old man or old lady,* at least that's the way we were taught at our house. Teachers were to be respected by the children they taught. They didn't wear sloppy attire in the classroom, sit on the desktop to teach or hang around with the high school *kids* outside of school hours.

While visiting a high school one day during change of classes time, young folks were going this way and that while running into each other and cramming the hallway. Remember when we were instructed to always walk on the *right side* of the hallway? It was a simple yet effective way of managing the change of classes; also useful in driving down the highway. Keep to the right; no clutter, no wrecked cars. It occurred to me the administration may be uncomfortable about making hallway rules between classes. Maybe the young folks wouldn't like it.

Perhaps we won't know unless we try.

Life is full of rules to make living easier. How hard can it be to follow them?

Remember *table manners*?

Men do not wear a hat at the table.

Offer the food to the older person at the table first, or to the guest.

If you don't care for the dish that's passed to you, the response is *no, thank you*; not, *I don't like that*.

When you were ready to leave the table you asked to be excused.

Like this; "May I be excused?" (Mom or Dad would acknowledge your departure.)

Of course this scenario of the family at the dinner table may not be a starting place for manners or conversation in the home these days.

Everyone is busy being busy.

Times have changed. The dinner table has disappeared.

Rules can be frustrating; changing rules to suit the times doesn't always help the situation.

Laws are meant to be obeyed. If you don't like them, there is a way to work toward having them legally changed. Everyone doesn't think or believe the way we do.

Let's talk about it.

I was watching a commercial yesterday as a young girl is screaming at her Mother, *"I'm not hungry."* Poor Mother, she's chasing the kid down the hall with a dish and a spoon. She simply must find something the dear child likes. Macaroni and cheese in a package is the answer. The kid gobbles it up.

When I was a child, (remember it was the forties and fifties), I was told, *"If you don't want to eat what's on the table, you may be excused. Maybe you'll be hungry again at the next meal."* No snacks in between, no dessert unless you eat what's put before you first.

As I watched that commercial, I found myself wondering how many little kids were watching it. Little kids don't understand the *advertising ways* of the world of television. They think it's the *real* thing; everybody does it.

Do we?

What's with all this *"protest"* stuff? Are you mad because the town, the state, the country has done something you don't like. *Protest!* Tear it down! Set it on fire! Throw paint on it! Start your own town! Throw stones at the police! Get rid of the police! Destroy businesses! Break their glass windows! Set police cars on fire! Scream the *"f"* word in everyone's face.

If you aren't old enough to vote, you may have to wait until your voice can be heard at the ballot box. That is, if *the box* is still in use. There seems to be a difference of opinion in some areas about circulating ballots to all the names on the list whether or not they've been requested, through the mail. Our voices may become completely lost in the process.

In case it has gone unnoticed, much of what we need to learn begins at home. No, the kids don't get to do everything they desire. When we find ourselves saying, *"My parents would never have put up with that."* Well,guess who the parents are now. That's us. That's Mom and Dad. Manners don't drop out of the sky. Rules around home don't come with your birth certificate. Choices are made by the parents. This is the way we do it *at our house.*

Cell phones don't own us. At least, they aren't supposed to own us.

Sitting in a restaurant one day, I watched two folks highly engrossed in their phones, sitting across the table but seemingly not aware of the presence of each other.

Is that what you call going out for coffee, or a coke, or what?

When I was a young person, my favorite movies had actors like Roy Rogers, and Gene Autry. No violence. It's a challenge today to find something on television that doesn't contain violence or sex. The kids are watching it too, folks. Maybe we should pay more attention to what they're doing with their time. How long has it been since your kids have heard, *"go outside and play"?*

Even the very little ones, as soon as they can sit up without help, are watching the television.

I don't know what Mom and Dad are doing, but they aren't watching the kids. Does anyone read to their young children anymore? You don't have time, you say?

Well find the time!

There! I think I feel better now. At least for the moment, I do.

But, I'll be back..

Count on it!

MOMENTS OF THE DAY

I Saw An Eagle Today
From My Porch Swing
A Moment In Time

I Saw An Eagle Today

Sun is shining; Sky is blue,

Everyone's busy, free moments few.
Economy's rising, dollar holds true.

I Saw An Eagle Today

Church pews half empty, more folks at the store.
Few cars on the highway,
Been here before.

I Saw An Eagle Today

Some feel lonely this time of year.
Laughter and family, for them, disappear.
Doesn't seem right without happiness here.

I Saw An Eagle Today

Why does it seem like today passed me by?
Yesterday's memories cannot tell me why.

Tomorrow will bring me another blue sky.

I Saw An Eagle Today

Today, as I left the church service,
My eyes were drawn to the sky.

At just that moment, an American Bald Eagle flew over.
Those who know me have often heard me say,
"Any day I see an eagle is a perfect day for me."

As the day wore on, blue moments overtook me.
Time and again the picture in my mind
Was of the soaring eagle I'd seen that morning.

Early evening approached.
It was then I realized
I'd had the perfect day,
Thanks to the beautiful moment this morning.

I Saw An Eagle Today

From My Porch Swing

Through the years there's been a view which never seems to change.
Spindly trees and weed filled fields greeted us when first we came to live.
In sixty years, or more, we've changed so much, my mate and me; and now my view
is filled with giant trees and brush.
I didn't see it happening.

Across the road, where once our sons and neighbor children came to play, on
stubby fields of meadow grass, the trees and underbrush have grown so high no
pathways show.

Still, even now, those little boys and girls seem ever young. I'm filled with joyful
memories of them playing there.

Hidden among the trees and brush, in memory, there lies that open meadow.
Joyful youth play games once more on long, hot summer days in full pursuit of life.

The days and nights and sounds of living never left my inner soul. Returning often
to this quiet place, from my porch swing I relive those treasured days of years gone
by.

Gently swinging, deep in thought, memories return. I recall each day with love.

The days begin at summer's dawn and end with muffled, evening sounds.

Nothing troubles, thoughts abound, peace is found.
From My Porch Swing

A MOMENT IN TIME. . .AT THE END OF THE DAY

1995

Readily identifiable sounds of geese
could be heard as they flew over our home.

Trees formed a thick canopy of leaves over the place where we sat on our
porch swing. We could hear the geese, yet couldn't see them clearly.

One glimpse of them through the hanging leaves,
told us there were five.

Our farm spans twenty acres, eight of which are hay fields. Geese often head
toward them, on a late summer day to feed and rest before starting the long
journey south for the winter.

As the five flew over our yard,
a fluffy white feather floated quietly to the ground.

What were the chances that a tiny feather
could find its way
through the crowded leaves,
coming to rest on the grass before us?

I began to think of the way we are linked together
through His creation.

The markings of the geese are specific,
always the same for a particular breed.

Our family has lived on this aging farm
for more than sixty years. On a quiet August evening
we had decided to rest
on the porch swing
enjoying a quiet time.

At that moment,
our Maker placed us together, in a unique way,
with other creatures of His creation.

He is the One
who all the oceans placed,
set the world in space
and created... "us".

Now,
He has chosen to join His creations together

for a special moment in time.

Coincidence? Perhaps...

Winging low across the evening sky,

with necks outstretched,

the five in line responded to imprinted flight

formed countless centuries ago.

A canopy of leaves formed overhead,

blocking them from view.

Gliding lower, wings now set,

the five flew toward feeding fields at dusk.

How quickly they had come into our solitude;

disappearing into evening shadows.

Out of sight, ghostly silhouettes,

markings meticulously ordained when time began.

A snow white feather drifted slowly to the ground;

Now cradled in the grass,

The evening dew its bed.

Binding our lives with theirs,

All, now ever changed.

The great creative plan of One

who set the world in space,

the oceans placed, species defined,

now paused with us for a moment in time.

We were one with Him.

It was the end of the day.

Begins and Ends At Home

The Doorway To My Memories

My Lasting Impression Of Mary
On Her Way To Eternal Life

The Doorway To My Memories

"Memories exploded as I stood in the doorway"

It was the early seventies; our congregation was considering the possibility
of constructing
a new church building.

The building at The Heights in Houghton Lake was old and too small for the
growing congregation. In addition, the basement often flooded in the spring of the
year.   Sunday School class attendance was increasing. The choir was small but
more singers were starting to join.
Our neighboring town   had recently built a beautiful new church.

A committee in our church, seeking ideas, was formed.

*"Let's go to West Branch
and check out their new building."*
Of course I wanted to be on that committee.

The new church was in my former home town.
Any excuse to re-visit the memories of my youth, was a great idea.

I was thirty-three at the time.

The new United Methodist Church in West Branch
was built on the County Farm property
across the street
from the house where I'd lived
until I was seventeen.

If you've read in my articles,
"Banished But Not Forever"
you have some idea of my emotional attachment
to the County Farm.
I have many memories of the wonderful lady, Mrs. Kelly,
who was my friend.

As the others wandered the hallways, looking at the possibilities for our new
church,
I decided to take a little side trip. Toward the end of a hallway, there was an exit
door.

Standing quietly, staring out the door, long forgotten memories were suddenly returning.

I'd stood in this place many times.

It appeared to me as though this doorway was exactly where the entrance to Mrs. Kelly's kitchen had been.   I had entered through it many times when visiting my friend.

It really didn't matter if the building's blueprints showed my estimate of the location to be incorrect. This was a view I'd seen many times before. *(Was that the aroma of homemade bread?)*

* * * * *

Still today,
when in town, I often drive into the former County Farm parking area and set for a few minutes; remembering.

The location of this beautiful   church, offers me memories of pleasant days gone by.

There was and is,
an oil well pump on the East side of the parking lot.
The old barn bridge is often visible, depending on the time of year and how many leaves are remaining on the trees.

The barn is gone, but remains in memory, as does the chicken coop and the pasture where the sheep were kept.
I remember Mr. Kelly
driving his team past our house
on his way to the hay fields. One time, after his daughter had gone away to college, he let me drive the old truck while he brought in the hay from the fields. I loved it.

Next door,
at the North end of the parking area,
is the West Branch Township Hall.

It hasn't aged.

(I have...a little.)

* * * *

On the day of our committee's visit,
I could feel emotion rising in my throat. Glad I was standing at the door to my
memories alone; I couldn't have spoken to anyone right then.

Memory was taking me back
to a time in my life
of great happiness and joy.

As we were returning to our home town,
I casually mentioned to my fellow travelers my experience standing by the door at
the end of the hall.

No one seemed overwhelmed by my revelations.
(Should they have been? Probably not.)

A few days later,
traveling to a meeting in another town with my Dad,
I began to share my experience
of the treasured memories of the County Farm and the return of them while visiting
at the doorway of the church.

Once again, I found it difficult to speak.

Regaining my composure,
I shared with my Dad my emotions at the time.
He listened attentively; then began to share his thoughts with me.

*"Most people encounter experiences such as you had,
as they grow older and their lives have changed,"* he said.
*"They remember the joys of youth.
They remember folks who were important to them who have either passed on or
are no longer living nearby."*

*"Buildings they remember have often been removed by deterioration
or replaced by new construction."*

*"You are young
to be having such memories overtake you."*

* * * *

Today, when I'm visiting the town of my youth,

I'm still making memories.

The doorway to my future is open.

Life for me is still experienced
one day at a time

Have you stood in a doorway of memories lately?

My Lasting Impression Of Mary

They always appeared just before the service began.
He carried a small pillow under his arm; I always wondered why.
Together they sat in the front pew, listening attentively.

One Sunday, as the service ended, Mary's husband stood to leave. I noticed the
pillow he had carried under his arm now lay on the church pew where he had
placed it to sit upon. the pillow showed two dents from his hipbones.

A World War 1 veteran, Don had been gassed during the time of his service to our
country. He was frail and attentive and attended the worship service with Mary
every Sunday.

I would never have known Mary had it not been for attending the same church as
she and her husband, Don. She was a faithful worshiper; together they entered the
sanctuary each Sunday.

Always leaving quietly, without conversation, they offered a nod and smiles to those
who greeted them.

Mary was a tall woman and on Sunday morning she was always attired in her
Sunday best. In winter, a bandanna around her head saved her from the cold and
rain. Old-fashioned rubber boots protected her from the elements when necessary.

Mary would never know the lasting impression she made on my life, and surely
upon the lives of others. Her faithful love of the Lord, deep affection for her
husband and two sons, and respect for the flag of our country were lessons for
many, if they would only observe.
She never served on a committee at church, but attended every meeting. Having
no vehicle, she walked the distance to the church from her home, a mile away at
the time.

One special meeting was scheduled to discuss the building of a new church. It was
held on a summer evening. We gathered in the basement of our old church and
Mary, as always, was there.

The idea of our small congregation taking on this large project had been discussed
for some time. During a moment of quiet in the meeting, Mary reached in her old
worn purse, pulling out a wrinkled bill. As she laid it on the table, she said;

"There's your first dollar".
The project was under way.

One January morning, public church services were cancelled due to a blizzard. It was dangerous to ask the parishioners to venture into the storm.

I felt warm and cozy as I sat in my living room watching a few cars driving down the highway a short distance away.
Then I saw Mary.
She was walking toward the church, carrying her Bible.
The ever-present cold weather scarf was tied under her chin. Her long wool coat offered protection from the blowing snow.
I felt ashamed.
I didn't live as far from the church as Mary.
I had a car.
Mary was walking.
I was relaxing in my nice warm house.

The scene has stayed with me for many years.

Recalling another dreary day, as I was driving home, I saw Mary walking in the heavy rain. Carrying her Bible, she was headed in the direction of her home.
I stopped to give her a ride and asked her where she'd been.
"I was at a Bible study at the church", she said.

As she climbed our of my car in front of her house, the rain was increasingly heavy.
Thanking me for the ride, she walked over to their flagpole; carefully retrieving our American flag from the pouring rain.
She folded it, and took it into her house.

Mary's favorite saying was;
"God knows all about it".
Reverend Jim once commented,
*"If it were possible to ride into heaven on someone's coattails,
I'd choose Mary."*

I always hoped that Mary would have enough room on those coattails
for me.

On Her Way To Eternal Life

Unattractive, Uneducated, Uninformed.

Not practiced at correctness,

Mary lived her life

One

Simple

Uncomplicated day

At a time.

Never indulging in self-satisfaction,

Nor pursued by dreams of personal success,

Her simple life was unadorned with expectations.

Knowing no pretense

Mary cast her lot

With God.

God first, Love, Worship, Prayer, Service

Family second, Love, Prayer, Care, Service

Country third, Love, Service, Prayer, Respect

No unexpected event

No shortfall

No misfortune

Could cause her simple faith

To waver.

"God knows all about it," Mary would say.

Her countenance always displayed

Unflappable peace.

Mary's life was uneventful,

Her faith unshakable.

Her example unforgettable.

Never doubting the unquenchable supply

Of God's love and care,

Mary lived to the fullest

The abundant life

Of a saint.

Her legacy to those who knew her

Was a trail of unerring discipleship;

On her way to eternal life with God.

March 31, 1996

FOOD FOR THOUGHT

Monday Morning At The Coffee Shop
Questions
He's Waiting For You
Where Is Your Heart?
All Things Are Possible
There Is A River
The Shepherd Called Them Home

The Shepherd Called Them Home

The quaint old man in knee high boots prepared to call them in...

"Get behind the barn," he said. "If they see you they won't come."

"How many sheep?" I asked.

'Bout 300, lambs 'n all," was his reply.

He gestured now toward distant fields,

no movement was revealed.

Obligingly, I took my place behind the aging barn.

Waiting, watching as I hid, chuckling as I did his bidding.

Toward a crumbling fence he moved, following a trampled path.

Now he stood near leaning gate and I began my wait.

With steady steps, he walked and called;

No words escaped his weathered lips, just eerie, high toned wailing sounds known only to his flock.

Behind the barn I waited.

Around the side I peeked and looked toward leaning gate.

All I saw were endless fields.

He stood alone to wait.

Suddenly a far off hill was filled with moving masses.

Then, out of sight, no movement seen,

A quiet moment passes.

Beyond the hill and nearer now, racing through the fields,

The flock now moves as one,

toward Him,

who waited, calm and still.

His presence did not yield.

Three hundred creatures fell in line

behind the One

whose voice they knew.

Through the gate, into the fold, now safe at last.

The Shepherd brought them home.

"Where your treasure is, there will your heart be also." (Matt:6:21)

Monday Morning At The Coffee Shop

The Pharisees are investigating the healing of the blind man.
(John 9:13-34)

Pharisee #1 - *"The jerk who just came in says he was blind but now he can see".*

Pharisee #2 - *"Nothing is that simple."*

Pharisee #1 - *"Well, ya know what they say. If it seems too good to be true, it probably isn't."*

Pharisee #2 - *" The guy must have done something really bad to be blind in the first place."*

Pharisee #1 - *"Probably his father was blind. They say the apple never falls far from the tree."*

Jesus (Sitting at the Counter) - *"I just healed the man as my Father led me."*

Pharisee #1 -*"Well that was quite a lucky break for the guy, you healing him. Just who do you think you are anyway?"*

Jesus - *"You'll have to take my word for who I am."*

Pharisee #2 - *"Hey mister! Who's responsible for healing your blindness?"*

The Former Blind Man - *"A man called Jesus."*

Pharisee #1 - So where is this guy now?"

The Former Blind Man - *"He's sitting right over there at the counter."*

Pharisee #2 - *"Let's just let the law handle it."*

LAWMAN TO FORMER BLIND MAN - *"Buddy, you've been traveling on a restricted license because of your blindness. You haven't been wearing your seatbelt either. You'd better come clean about this cured blindness. What's going on*

72

here?"

The Former Blind Man - "All I know for sure is that I was blind and he helped me to see."

Pharisee #1 - "So what is he, a doctor?"

Pharisee #2 - "Call the guy's parents."

Blind Man's Dad - "He's ours alright. But he's a big boy so he can speak for himself."

Pharisee #1 - "If that _Jesus_ guy is a doctor, I'd call him a quack!"

The Former Blind Man -"For a couple of guys with so many questions, you sure don't have many answers. When I tell you what happened, you don't listen to me."

Pharisee #2 - "Hit the road buddy. Your kind never changes."

Pharisee #1 - "How much do we owe ya for the coffee, lady?

* * *

Questions

How difficult to think of Him
As merely man.

Did He have cabin fever
In mid-winter too?

Was He reflective,
After spending time with folks
Because of things He said,
Or didn't say?

Did someone need to talk with Him
While He hurried
On His way?

Was He discouraged by the weather?

Was He tempted to make bread from stones?
The Bible says He was.
Does that mean when I'm tempted
I am not alone?

Will God be in my heart and head
If I listen well to Him
And learn his teachings?

Starting now,
Is there still time?
Was time His enemy?

Is it mine?

Did He finish all His daily chores
And wake at night
Wishing He'd accomplished more?

If I could gain acclaim
With talents given me by God,
Would I, as He
Refuse the moment's gain
For certain pain?

I wonder if He knew
That I would question
If He really understood
The little things
That happen in my day?

He said He would.

He's Waiting For You

(That night, Paul had a dream. A Macedonian stood on the far shore and called across the sea. "Come over to Macedonia and help us!" The dream gave Paul his map...we knew now for sure that God had called us to preach the good news to the Europeans.) Acts 16.9(The Message)

The world of Paul seems far from ours.

Today, the television brings the world into our living rooms.

The good news, the bad news and news that isn't news at all

Invades our lives

every day.

Paul believed God was sending him to preach in Macedonia.

God was calling him.

Now, the planet earth can be seen from a camera on a satellite

revolving through space.

Through the lens of a camera

carried by a robot,

We can watch as the moon is explored.

With a computer,

a phone line, a connection to the Internet,

We can visit with someone who lives in France or Greece,

send them a picture of ourselves,

communicate with them.

We will never meet them;

However, it is possible to maintain a friendship with these persons in far off lands.

One may inhabit an operating room in Australia

through a camera fixed in position

as a human heart is removed,

repaired and replaced

in fine condition,

into the body of a man

whose name we will never know.

Why would we pay any attention to a dream like Paul's,   or a vision,

when life in the this century

has so much to offer?

As children we were warned,

"Don't let your imagination run away with you."

"Learn to be sensible and realistic."

"Keep your feet on the ground".

Could the God of the Bible become a real part of our lives?

The Apostle Paul believed the Holy Spirit could speak to him in

his own affliction,

his thorn in the flesh.

That was Paul, not us.

As time passes, God's message will become clear to us.

We will hear it through the timely witness of a friend,

the words of a song,

a recommended book,

an inner urge

to learn and experience

this thing call Christianity.

There will be new opportunities to serve Him in the church.

There will be continuing revelations of an elusive "something more".

The God of the universe will become personal to us.

The good news is that He cares for us..

He knows our names and all about our lives.

He knows our deepest and most private thoughts.

He knows the unspoken desires of our hearts.

In John 5:1-9 (*The Message*)

While Jesus was visiting Jerusalem for one of the Jewish religious holidays,

He came to the Sheep Gate near the Bethesda Pool.

It was here where crowds of sick people waited for a miraculous healing

by entering the stirring waters of the pool.

One of the men by the pool, who had been sick for 38 years,

came into Jesus' view.

Jesus asked him, *"Would you like to get well?"*

What an interesting question for Jesus to ask the man.

Hadn't he been coming to this pool every day

in order to be made whole?

He had been crippled for 38 years;

of course he wanted to be healed.

The man responded that he couldn't be healed

since he had no one to help him into the pool.

He believed that it was the fault of his friends

who hadn't helped him,

that he had been unable to be healed.

Jesus said to the man,

"Stand up, roll up you're sleeping mat and go home."

Instantly the man was healed.

The word of God became personal and real to him.

The moment comes

when it's time to move

from where we are

to where He wants us to be.

The Holy Spirit speaks to us in our condition

while living at home, attending our church and living in our world.

The move must be made unassisted.

Are you where He wants you to be?

Have you experienced the vision?

Is the Holy Spirit using a time in your life

to call you to witness for Him?

Have you heard the message from God?

You there,

get up, pick up your sleeping mat.

Step into the stirring, healing waters of life

in Jesus Christ.

HE'S WAITING FOR YOU

Where Is Your Heart?

"Where your treasure is, there will your heart be also"   Matt:6:21

Did you offer to release something for the Lenten season this year?

Do you remember what it was?

Was it a cherished possession
you've always dreamed of owning
and handing down to your children?

Perhaps it was a particular item you needed
in order to complete a collection.

Now you were giving it away.

Was it an object you've desired to own for years?

Could it have been an item

in which you'd lost interest?

In the Gospel of Mark, a man comes running to Jesus,
kneels down before Him and asks;

"What must I do to get to heaven?" Jesus answers, *"You know the commandments,
don't kill, don't commit adultery, don't steal, don't lie,*

always respect your Father and your Mother."

The man replies, *"Teacher, I've never broken a single one of those laws."*

Scripture tells us that Jesus felt genuine love for the man.

He said to him,

"You only lack one thing, go and sell all that you have

and give the money to the poor,

and you shall have treasure in heaven."

A difficult thing was required of the man.

A difficult thing is also required of you and me.

So then what is required?

Would we give up our home
in order for a poor family to have a place to live?

Would we give up our annual vacation
in order to give our employer
the opportunity to give our
vacation pay
to a person who has no employment?

Would we transfer our civil rights
to someone who has none,

such as an illegal immigrant?

Jesus told his disciples,

*"It is easier, easier for a camel to go through the eye of a needle
than for a rich man to enter the Kingdom of Heaven?"*

The disciple, in turn, exclaimed,

"Then who can enter and be saved

if a rich man cannot?"

Who is a rich man? What makes him rich?

Jesus suggests that the things we treasure most
are the things that make us rich.
Those things are our homes,
our parents, our brothers and sisters,

our children and our property.

Are we willing to give up those things
for the privilege of entering heaven?

Jesus tells us we will be rewarded one hundred times over

with the same things we willingly gave away.

We do this for the love of God

and for the privilege
of being able to share with others

the Good News of the Gospel.

In addition to receiving such abundant rewards,

we will also receive persecutions.

In spite of them, in the world to come
we shall have eternal life.

The Christian walk has many twists and turns.

What things then, are to be desired?

God asked Abraham to sacrifice his son, Isaac, as a burnt offering.

Abraham was willing to obey.

In Genesis 22 the angel of the Lord told Abraham

to stop and not hurt the boy.

"For I know that God is first in your life.

You have not even withheld your beloved son."

Is God first in my life?
Is He first in yours?

Will God wait for us
as we take these faltering steps
to become closer to Him?

How many times will God forgive us
when we don't quite measure up?

"I" should have made that phone call.

"You" should have stopped to visit that person.

Why didn't *"I"* send that card?

Why did *"you"* refuse when you were asked to serve
on a committee at church?

We said, *"Ask someone else".*

Someone else was asked

and someone served God
in the place that had been offered to *us.*

Do *we* sometimes wonder
if that person will take *our* place
at the gates of heaven?

Wonderful treasures are all around *us...*

everywhere *we* look...

every day of *our* lives.

From Scripture,
a line in the Gospel of Matthew seems appropriate.

"Where your treasure is,

there will your heart be also."
(Matthew 6:21)

Where is your treasure?

Did you know that your heart is there also?

Your heart is the very thing that gives you life.

Is your heart and treasure with Jesus?

All Things Are Possible

"What this adds up to, then, is this. No more lies, no more pretense. Tell your neighbor the truth. In Christ's body we are all connected to each other, after all. When you lie to others, you end up lying to yourself."

"Watch what God does, and then you do it, like children who learn proper behavior from their parents."(The Message)

The question is, am I a part of the body of Christ?

I attend church somewhat regularly. I pray sometimes but maybe not as often as I could or should. I joined the church. I sing songs in the church. I give some of my money to the church. I've been baptized. Do these things I have done make me a part of the body of Christ?

Are my sins forgiven? How do I know if I have the Holy Spirit?

These were the questions the gathered brothers asked Peter in the book of Acts.2:37. So now what do we do?

Peter said, *"Change your life. Turn to God and be baptized. Do this each of you in the name of Jesus Christ, so your sins are forgiven. Receive the gift of the Holy Spirit. The promise is targeted to you and your children. (The Message)*

I admit there are times when I'm tired of being me. I'm tired of experiencing defeat. I'm tired of feeling guilty and alone. I wonder if I'll ever reach the point of trusting Jesus Christ so much that I want Him to take control of me? Am I ready to live that kind of life? If I am ready, what happens then?

"I must know Jesus Christ as my lord and Savior before His teaching has any meaning for me. Other than that (it's just) a lofty ideal which only leads to despair. But when I am born again by the Holy Spirit of God, I know that Jesus Christ did not come only to teach. He came to make me what he teaches me to be. Jesus says..."Then you're in a wonderful place, let me show you how it's done". *(My Utmost For His Highest-Oswald Chambers)*

Chambers)

It is good to work against racism even if one should fail. It is good to work against poverty even though the poor will always be with us. These things are so because a moral choice and moral actions reflecting God's nature are good in themselves, whether or not they are successful.

"No one can make himself pure by obeying laws. Jesus Christ does not give us rules and regulations. He gives us His teachings, which are truths that can only be interpreted by His nature, which He places within us. This comes from the indwelling of the Holy Spirit." Chambers continues; *"The great wonder of Jesus Christ's salvation is that He changes our heredity He does not change our human nature. He changes its source. He doesn't change our natural instincts. He replaces them. Our new instincts come from Him. And with these new instincts He changes our motives as well." (My Utmost For His Highest-Oswald Chambers)*

When we've accepted Jesus Christ as our Lord and Savior, the source becomes the Holy Spirit within us.

"Beware of thinking of our Lord as only a teacher. If Jesus Christ is only a teacher, then all He can do is frustrate me by setting a standard before me I cannot attain. What is the point of presenting me with such a lofty ideal if I cannot possible come close to reaching it?" (My Utmost For His Highest-Oswald Chambers)

The answer is, I must commit my life to Him and receive His Spirit.

Chambers reminds us; *"There is only one master of the human heart; God, not religion." (My Utmost For His Highest-Oswald Chambers)*

Have we ever considered the business of being religious might get in our way of having a relationship with God? In a way, religion can become our God. Who or perhaps what, is the master of my heart?

In Matthew 6:24, Jesus reminded us of this. *"You cannot serve two gods at once. Loving one god, you'll end up hating the other". (The Message)*

This isn't the end of my quest. It doesn't end with asking Jesus Christ to become my own personal Lord and Savior. It doesn't end with the repenting of my sins and the committing of my life to Christ. It doesn't end at all.

It begins.

Who, or perhaps what, is the master of my heart? So what's the point? We have not arrived at this place solely to develop a spiritual life of our own. We are here to take part and to be a part in the building of Christ's body, the church. We are joined to one another in Him. As the scripture reminds us, we are all connected to each other.

One step at a time and one day at a time, God reveals to us His purpose for each of us in His Body. Absolute obedience to His spirit is required. We are to be used to complete His plan, His purpose, and not our own. In the process, the fruits of our obedience will be revealed within his perfect plan.

God has given us free will. We can choose to be obedient or we can choose to follow our own inclinations and desires.

In effect, we can choose to be our own God.

In Mark 8, Jesus says; " *Anyone who intends to come with me has to let me lead. You're not in the driver's seat, I am. What good would it do to get everything you want and lose (yourself), the real you? What could you ever trade your soul for?" (The Message)*

We are quite familiar with the concept of obedience. We've known since childhood the results of both obedience and disobedience. We are familiar with the rules and regulations of the highway, the state, and the country. We know the price to be paid for disobedience to those rules and regulations.

In America, we are free to challenge our government's laws.

We can appeal the decisions of the courts when we disagree with their judgments. Sometimes we can get a law changed. We can question the meaning of our laws and hire an attorney to argue our position for us if necessary.

It is the duty of the Court to interpret the meaning of the laws which the founders had in mind when they penned the Constitution of the United States.

Currently there are many questions revolving around our government's constitution and its original intent.

Was the United States of America founded on Christian principles? Were the writers of the constitution Christians? Was the United States of America founded as a Christian state?

If it was, does that mean all other religions were to be excluded?

I suggest to you the Holy Spirit, which abides in us, will lead us through the discourses of today as well as the discourses of the scriptures.

The Bible is a living book with revelations of life on every page waiting for us to discover its meanings to us and to our world. The Spirit is our guide.

The sermon on the mount dealt with all aspects of living the Christian life. Among them were being and doing. Matthew 7: (*The Message*) *"Don't look for shortcuts to God. The market is flooded with surefire, easygoing formulas for a successful life that can be practiced in your spare time."*

"Don't fall for that stuff, even though crowds of people do.....The way of life to God is vigorous and requires total attention."

"Be wary of false preachers who smile a lot, dripping with practiced sincerity. Chances are they are out to rip you off some way or other. Don't be impressed with charisma, look for character. Who preachers are is the main thing, not what they say. A genuine leader will never exploit your emotions or your pocketbook."

"These diseased trees with their bad apples are going to be chopped down and burned. Knowing the correct password and saying Master Master, for instance, isn't going to get you anywhere with God. What is required is serious obedience, doing what my Father wills."

"I can see it now at the final judgment. Thousands will be strutting up to me and saying, Master we preached the message, we bashed the demons, our God sponsored projects had everyone talking. And do you know what I am going to say? You missed the boat. All you did was use me to make yourselves important. You don't impress me one bit."

"These words I speak to you are not incidental additions to your life. They are not homeowner improvements to your standard of living. You're out of here. These are foundational words to build a life on."

"If you work these words into your life, you're like a smart carpenter who built his house on a solid Rock. Rain poured down, the river flooded, a tornado hit. But nothing moved that house. It was fixed to the rock. But if you just use my words in Bible studies and don't work them into your life, you are like a stupid carpenter who built his house on the sandy beach. When a storm rolled in and the waves came up it collapsed like a house of cards."

Continuing Matthew 5:33-37 (*The Message*).."*And don't say anything you don't mean. This counsel is embedded deep in our traditions. You only make things worse when you lay down a smoke screen of pious talk, saying "I'll pray for you," and never doing it. Or saying, "God be with you" and not meaning it."*

"You don't make your words true by embellishing them with religious lace. In making your speech sound more religious it becomes less true. When you manipulate words to get your own way, you go wrong."

And again in *Matthew*: "*Be especially careful when you're trying to be good so that you don't make a performance out of it. It might be good theater, but the God who made you won't be applauding. And when you come before God, don't turn that into a theatrical production either. All these people making a regular show out of their prayers, are hoping for stardom."*

"Let me tell you why you are here. You're here to be salt-seasoning that brings out the God-flavors of this earth. If you lose your saltiness, how will people taste godliness? You've lost your usefulness and will end up in the garbage. Here's another way to put it. You're here to be light, bringing out the God colors in the world. God is not a secret to be kept." (The Message)

You and I are here to *BE* the body of Christ.

John Wesley put it quite simply, "*Do all the good you can, by all the means you can, in all the ways you can, in all the places you can, at all the times you can, to all the people you can, as long as ever you can.*"

Watching what God does and trying to do the same is a full time endeavor. Through the indwelling presence of the Holy Spirit, through the church the body of Christ, all things are possible.

Quotations from

"The Message"

My Utmost For His Highest- (Oswald Chambers)

There Is A River

There is a river, a canal of sorts, bordering a highway near my home. Ducks and geese may often be seen on it as well as a few swans inhabiting the backwaters nearby.

Many years ago, spindly willow saplings were planted beside the canal; eventually, as was the plan, the young trees became a barrier to save vehicles from sliding into the water.

One rarely notices the slow growth of a tree and over the years the little saplings seemed to quickly become mature trees; hanging over the edge of the canal. The water was the source for their growth; for a time, they all grew well. As the years passed, the trunks became broken and the trees disintegrated into heaps of tangled brush.

Willows, when planted within distance of water, grow to be magnificent. After a time, they become troublesome.
The willow could be called a dirty tree, as it drops its twigs and branches on the ground beneath.
It grows tall and thick and when near an abundant water source it may literally consume a large area beneath.
The fruit of the trees are the twigs and branches it continually drops on the ground to rot.
The roots are constantly seeking water and will search and settle for any available moisture.

My roots, too, are constantly searching for nourishment. God created me with a longing within to find and return to Him. He has provided me with a Way.
Through His word, through His Son, and through the indwelling of the Holy Spirit, my nourishment may be found. He offers every thing needed. It's available to everyone.
In Matthew 5, (The Message)
"This is what God does.
He gives His best, the sun to warm and the rain to nourish, to everyone, regardless:
the good and bad, the nice and nasty."

So everyone gets the rain, the good and the bad, the flower and the weed, the nice and the nasty. What happens after that depends upon my search for His nourishment and the determined persistence in my God given roots.

In Jeremiah 17:7,8 (The Message)
" Blessed is the man, who trusts me, God,
the woman who sticks with God,
they're like trees replanted in Eden,
putting down roots near the rivers...never a worry through the hottest of summers,
never dropping a leaf, serene and calm through droughts,
bearing fresh fruit every season.

Mankind was designed to be as fruit bearing trees with roots in God's Kingdom and with faith in His Son, Jesus Christ; not as the willow tree, dropping leaves and twigs and weakened branches with fruit to be used only for kindling.

Where am I finding my nourishment? Are the roots I've established bearing good fruit or disposable kindling? Am I so far away from my roots that I don't pay attention to where they are getting nourishment?
Perhaps I wont realize the quality of the source until I see the fruits of the harvest.

Recently, a message appeared on the internet, which was originally aired nationally in 1996 by Paul Harvey a well-known commentator of that time.
While not word for word accurate, this is a fair transcription of an actual prayer delivered before the Kansas House of Representatives by Central Christian Church Pastor Joe Wright, who was chaplain that day.

See what you think. The prayer went as follows;

Heavenly Father, we come before you today to ask your forgiveness and to seek
your direction and guidance.
We know your word says, "Woe to those who call evil Good," but that is exactly
what we have done".
We have lost our spiritual equilibrium and reversed our values.
We have exploited the poor and called it the lottery.
We have rewarded laziness and called it welfare.
We have killed our unborn and called it choice.
We have shot abortionists and called it justifiable.
We have neglected to discipline our children and called it building self-esteem.
We have abused power and called it politics.
We have coveted our neighbor's possessions and called it ambition.
We have polluted the air with profanity and pornography and called it freedom of
expression.

Search us, oh God, and know our hearts today; cleanse us from every sin and set us free. Amen"

Perhaps Jeremiah had something like this in mind; Chapter 17:9-10 *(The Message)*
"The heart is hopelessly dark and deceitful, a puzzle that no one can figure out. But I, God, search the heart and examine the mind. I get to the root of things. I treat them as they really are, not as they pretend to be."

What happens if God examine my mind and finds it to be dark and deceitful? What happens when God gets to my roots and treats them as they really are, and not as they pretend to be?

Luke 6:24 (*The Message*) has this to say,
"However, it's trouble ahead if you think you have it made. What you have is all you'll ever get. And it's trouble ahead if you're satisfied with yourself. Yourself will not satisfy you for long."
In Luke 6:26 *(The Message)*
"There's trouble ahead when you live only for the approval of others, saying what flatters them, doing what indulges them. Popularity contests are not truth contests. Look how many scoundrel preachers were approved by your ancestors! Your task is to be true, not popular."

To what source am I looking when I make my decisions? My decisions reinforce my strength or weaken it. Every day I make many life-changing decisions. They may not seem life changing at the time.
How do I know which way to turn? Who can tell me? Where can I find the answers?

The Methodist tradition teaches me to look for balance in four attributes of a decision.
They are:
First, is it based on Scripture? On all the scripture Old and New Testament.
That will help me to have a firm foundation for my decisions and choices, delivering me from the temptation to find a scripture that agrees with the decision I've already made.
(That form of decision-making is called proof texting. Don't be tempted to find a single text that proves your point of view.)

Second, is Tradition.

The tradition of the church throughout the ages means the church universal, small "c" and not just one particular denomination.

Third is Reason.

Is it reasonable?

Fourth is Experience.

Barclay's Commentary on the New Testament puts it this way;

"If a person tells you they've had an experience with Christ and it has changed their life, you cannot tell them that they haven't"

Experience through faith is important. It's real if it has changed your life. There is balance in these four equally important beliefs. With them, I may weigh in on the decisions I have to make.

There is strength here. There is strength in the Word of God.

Jeremiah 17:5 (The Message)

"Cursed is the strong one who depends on mere humans. Who thinks he can make it on muscle alone..and he sets God aside as dead weight. He's like a tumbleweed on the prairie out of touch with the good earth. He lives rootless and aimless in a land where nothing grows."

Tumbleweeds on the prairie drift along, pledging their love to the ground. They tumble here and there with the ever changing wind and are out of touch with the good earth. They are rootless and aimless in a land where nothing grows.

Mankind can never be free from longing to reach out and return to the God who created us. God has placed that longing in each of us at our conception, or before.

The truth is, my roots, which seem so far away from me are finding their nourishment from my choices in life.

Who and what has control of my Life?

Who and what has authority over my life?

In a devotional book by *Oswald Chambers*, titled *My Utmost For His Highest*, *Chambers writes this:*

Our Lord never insists on having authority over us.

He never says, "you will submit to me."

No, He leaves us perfectly free to choose.

So free, in fact, that we can spit in His face

Or we can put Him to death, as others have done;

And yet He will never say a word.

But once His life has been created in me through His redemption,

I instantly recognize His right to absolute authority over me.

He never insists on obedience,

But when we truly see Him
We will instantly obey.

What brings me to the point of realizing His right to absolute authority?

Chambers continues: "The knowledge of our own poverty is what brings us to the
proper place where Jesus Christ (can accomplish) His work."

In Luke 6:17-21 (The Message) Speaking about Jesus
"Coming down off the mountain with them,
He stood on a plain surrounded by disciples,
And was soon joined by a huge congregation
From all over Judea and Jerusalem,
Even from the seaside towns of Tyre and Sidon.
They had come both to hear Him and to be cured of their ailments.
Those disturbed by evil spirits were healed.
Everyone was trying to touch Him.
So much energy surging from Him,
So many people healed.
Then He spoke.
You're blessed when you've lost it all.
God's kingdom is there for the finding.
You're blessed when you're ravenously hungry,
Then you're ready for the Messianic meal.
You're blessed when tears flow freely.
Joy comes with the morning."

Chambers writes:
"The teaching of the Sermon on the Mount produces a sense of despair in the
natural person. Exactly what Jesus means for it to do. As long as we have some
self-righteous idea that we can carry out our Lord's teaching, God will allow us to
continue until we expose our own ignorance by stumbling over some obstacle in
our way. Only then are we willing to come to Him as paupers and receive Him."

Have I been calling evil good?
What have I accomplished in a society, a culture, a country?

Joy comes with the morning! Praise God!

94

When Did The Prejudice Creep In?

As the story goes, the little boy found a ladybug and was studying it quite intently. The Mother heard him say, *"It must be a gentleman bug"*. Questioning him as to why he seemed to know the opposite of "lady" was "gentleman" his response was, *"Because he's smart."* Mom wondered where he'd gotten the idea that gentleman were smart and ladies weren't. She wondered if she or the child's father had said something to have encouraged the child to reason that way. The only thing the Mother could think of was that she often said to the child, *"We'll have to ask Daddy when he comes home."*

As I read this little episode it caused me to question how prejudice and bias enters our lives.

What causes us to judge others; because of gender, color, wealth, good looks, or education? (Too much or too little of one or the other..)

I began to see that when we show partiality and prejudice, we are setting examples for our children..I am so thankful we have a heavenly Father who is no divider of persons,

He loves each one of us the same.

He desires that we in turn love one another with the same kind of love.

When I'm reminded of His unconditional and steadfast love, it helps me fight against the prejudice that tries to creep in and distort my conception of others.

Many years ago one of our sons, at the age of six, was circling toys in a catalogue that he would like to have for Christmas. He brought the book to me and pointed at an Easy Bake Oven. (Remember them?)

He asked me, *"Is this for a boy or a girl?"* I told him, *"If you like it, circle it."*

I was taken by surprise. At the tender age of six, he was afraid to say he liked something if someone would think the thing he liked was a "girl's toy".

We bought him the Easy Bake Oven that year, even though within a few months it was abandoned as a toy.

It's now 50 years later and I haven't forgotten the importance of his six year old question. *"Is it ok for me to like that?"*

For today's young people, the question may be *"Is it ok for Susie to want to pursue a degree in engineering?"* *"Is it ok for Kevin to want to be a nurse?"*

At the tender age of 6 our child was already concerned with what the "world" would think of him. And to be tagged as playing with a "girl's" toy was unthinkable. That was 50 years ago; a sad commentary on a child's world nestled within our adult world of prejudiced attitudes.

Attitudes are readily available to aid or detract from the forming of a child's dreams and goals in life.

In 1952, a movie was made of the life story of a gifted writer of fairy tales. His name was Hans Christian Anderson, and this movie was a musical. The part of Anderson was played by a wonderful actor of the time, Danny Kaye.

One of the songs that was sung, based on a children's story that Anderson had written, was called "The Ugly Duckling". That song, and Kay's unique rendition of it kept running through my mind as I prepared this article.

It was about...Prejudice...

I decided to investigate some of the facts about Hans Christian Anderson, the writer. This is what I found.

Anderson was raised in a Christian home by loving parents. He was known to be a gifted writer at an early age. The boy had a beautiful but very high voice until he was in his teens. He was an exceedingly homely young man at the age of 12. (He grew to be 6'1").

Anderson didn't fit society's requirements for a 12 year old boy. Children his own age didn't accept him, nor did the adults in his community. He was ridiculed and laughed at by the town people, although loved and nurtured at home.

I suspect the story about an Ugly Duckling is a reflection of his youth and the realization of his true worth as a grown man.

It's apparent to me, that even the natural world of animals and birds has prejudice;but their prejudice is instinctive.

Perhaps ours is also.

God has given us the ability to choose between our natural instincts and living our lives with the Spirit of Christ in our hearts.

Several years ago, I was privileged to hear a musical performed by a local Christian choir. The name of the presentation was "One Incredible Moment". And that moment was when God came to our world in the form of a human, a baby boy.

The baby was named Jesus.

As I listened to this beautiful performance, I found myself wondering,

when did the prejudice creep in?

No one seemed too upset by the event of his birth, except perhaps for King Herod. He would tolerate no intrusion on his power as ruler. So he proposed to have all the male children from birth to the age of 2, destroyed. He had them put to death.

The shepherds were pleased when the angel informed them of a child's birth. They were told the he was to be found in a lowly stable in Bethlehem. The angel's announcement to them on the hillside sent them joyously on their way to see the child who would be the Savior of the world.

No prejudice there.

And the Wise Men were willing to journey for two long years to find and worship a baby, an infant, a child.

No prejudice here.

When Jesus was 12 years old, he went to Jerusalem for the Feast of the Passover. When his parents arrived home, and discovered Jesus was not with them, they went back to Jerusalem and found him in the temple listening to the great teachers. He was asking them questions. The teachers didn't seem to mind the presence of this young child. They didn't mind his questions.

No one minded that this carpenter's child sat among the learned scholars in the temple. No one minded that he questioned them. No one minded that Jesus seemed to have a mind and a mission of his own.

WHEN DID THE PREJUDICE CREEP IN?

In the gospel of John, Chapter 1 verse 43, Jesus decides to leave Jerusalem for Galilee. Finding Phillip, he said to him, "Follow me. " Phillip, like Andrew and Peter, was from the town of Bethsaida.

Phillip found his friend, Nathaniel and told him, "We have found the one Moses wrote about in the Law. And about whom the prophets also wrote, Jesus of Nazareth, the son of Joseph".

"Nazareth?", Nathaniel asked, "Can anything good come from there?.

The prejudice seems to be starting.

I had the same reaction to something I said, several years ago, when I questioned a governing board as to why they had selected a local man, a professional person, to accomplish a task at hand. What I said was, (and I've thought long and hard about telling you this), *"If he's so good at what he does and so smart about what he knows, why is he doing business in this town instead of in the city where he could make more money?"*

I guess there's no doubt in your mind about *where* and into *whom* the prejudice crept in that time, is there?

Much as Phillip did, when Nathaniel asked *"Can anything good come out of Nazareth?"*, the gentle folk to whom I made that statement said to me.."*Why don't you come and see? This person has valid credentials and you'll find that his choice of a place to live has nothing to do with his ability to carry out his plan."*

WHY DID THAT PREJUDICE CREEP IN?

Where do our values come from? We listen, speak read, study and decide what to keep and what to throw away. We sort through and accept some things while rejecting others. We trust, believe, and follow something, someone.

Perhaps we think of ourselves more highly than we ought. Perhaps we think by putting others down, we set ourselves higher.

Perhaps we don't think at all.

As children, we absorb much from our families. We speak English because we hear English. If we were brought up in a home where Spanish or Russian was spoken, we would fluently speak those languages. When we speak our prejudices, our children hear and learn to speak our prejudices.

When we speak our faith our children hear and learn our faith, and desire to make it their own.

When we live in our prejudices, our children live their childhood years surrounded by our prejudices.

When we live our faith, our children live surrounded by the Christian love which our faith in Christ brings into our homes.

WHEN DO THE PREJUDICES CREEP OUT?

We would never have noticed them at all if Jesus hadn't come to live and to die to show us how wonderfully God loves us. Because of that wonderful gift of God's grace, sealed in the death and resurrection of His Son Jesus Christ, the gift of God's grace is ours...yours and mine, to accept and to begin to live a new life.

William Barclay, in his commentary, sums it up like this;

"It is not the force of man, but the love of God which alone can unite a disunited world".

When negative ways and attitudes, such as arrogance, contempt, condemnation and destructive thinking are cut off, "prejudice' has no fuel.

We don't know when the prejudice crept into our lives. We only know prejudice cannot co-exist with the love of Christ in our hearts and minds.

There is a story in the Bible about the woman who cleaned 7 demons out of her house, but she failed to fill her home with something else, and the demons moved back in and brought their friends with them.

It isn't enough to rid our lives of old and comfortable habits. Hearts, minds and lives filled with the love of Christ have no room for prejudice, arrogance, contempt, nor condemnation.

Our prejudices will turn into love.

Custom or Habit?

"He went to the synagogue, as was His custom"...

One day, when I was seventeen, my sister asked me to baby-sit with her infant son while they went out for the evening. I loved the little boy dearly.

The baby was suffering from a slight cold; my sister's instructions were to give him a spoon full of cough medicine from a bottle which she had left on the counter in the kitchen. When the time came to administer the cough syrup, I picked up the bottle, poured the medicine into a spoon and offered it to the baby.

As was my habit, my "usual behavior", I didn't bother to turn on the light in the kitchen.

The child immediately began to cough and cry, as he choked and spit out most of the medicine on his pajamas. This was not really an unusual response to bad tasting medicine, or so I thought. I turned on the light in the kitchen to assess the situation.

There was another small bottle on the counter. Upon checking, I saw that it contained the cough medicine.

The liquid I had poured into the spoon, was Tincture of Benzoin Compound, a substance used in vaporizers to help in easing breathing problems. Two bottles sat on the counter; without the light to show the names on the labels, I had chosen the wrong one.

I was devastated. This child who I dearly loved had nearly been poisoned by my irresponsible action. The little boy was fine. He suffered no ill effects from my carelessness, since most of the liquid had fallen on his pajamas.

Because of that experience, I have adopted a discipline; never administer or take a medication without first carefully checking the directions *in the light.*

This has become *my custom* and it has served me, and others, well, over time. It has become my *"practice of long standing."*

I was reading an explanation of a "parable", recently. The reference said Jesus often used parables for his listeners to quickly understand the point he was making. What idea would come into a person's mind when they heard the story he told them?

The article went on to say, the best thing to do to help a person, is to get them to think for themselves.

Is a *habit* the same as a *custom*?

The definition of the word, *habit*, is "a usual manner of behavior".

A "*custom*" (also called a tradition) is a common way of doing things.

When the *habit* of attending church becomes a tradition to us, we are ready to live; to worship and praise, to love and be loved, to listen and share His word within the congregation of believers on Sunday morning.

We are no longer burdened with a weekly decision; should I go or should I stay home? It's no longer a *usual manner*; it has become our *tradition*.

A study group with other Christians may now have become your tradition. Whether we join together on Sunday morning or another time during the week, we place ourselves in a position to grow and incorporate the meaning of His Word into our lives.

It has become, our tradition to listen, to learn, and to share.

Jesus, once again, has given us the example of His own life. *"He went to the synagogue, as was His (custom) tradition.*

Are your *habits* serving you well? Would you like to turn your *habits* into *traditions*? Your answer may be a life saver.

(*Lord;* " *Teach us Your ways. Help us to develop customs that will allow us to be used by You in Your ministries." Amen*)

***Note-The "child" is now in his seventies; in good health.*

A TRUE
MOUSE TALE

On my way home from a church meeting, one evening, I found myself thinking about the purpose and results of the meeting we'd just finished. We were discussing stewardship in the congregation. Someone said, "Maybe people don't understand what "stewardship" means". You'll just have to believe me when I tell you what happened next. Suddenly, there was a rather cute little mouse sitting on the dashboard of my car, and he began to talk to me about himself and plans for the future.

Jonathan Steward's Dream

"Let Me Introduce Myself", he said.

*I am not just a church mouse. I am not an ordinary field mouse. I am an
extraordinary Church Mouse.*

*I don't live in my church home by accident, mind you. I wanted a church for my
home and searched far and wide, at least a hundred feet in all directions; looking
for just the right location.*

Then one day, I saw it.

Standing before me was God's Church in Friendly Town by Beautiful Blue Lake.

*It's a very special privilege to live in God's Church. One can scarcely keep from
boasting about this wonderful home while attending mouse reunions, and mouse
conventions, and other mouse gatherings that only a mouse ever hears about.*

I know all about God; being a CMK.

*For those of you who've never heard of a CMK, I'll be happy to explain. There's
really nuthin' to it. It's just that my Daddy was a Church Mouse, my Granddaddy
was a Church Mouse and it sort of runs in our family.*

I'm just your average "C"hurch "M"ouse "K"id.

*I love every square inch of my church home, including the wastebasket in the
kitchen. There are all sorts of lovely crumbs there for me to snack upon. The
crumbs in the wastebasket in the Sunday school room are enjoyable too.
Sometimes there are special pieces of paper that help to line my nest. Let me tell*

you about the loose corner of the carpet at the back of the sanctuary.

I often lie there in my nest and listen to the pastor's sermon on Sunday morning.

There are many special places in my church home, like the hole in the plaster near the front door. Someone pounded a nail there to hang a wreath at Christmas time. Plaster crumbs help to make a sturdy floor in a mouse nest, you know.

One day, while I was resting behind the water fountain in the hallway, Mr. Green was carefully filling the nail hole with putty. He sanded it and painted over it so it looked just like the rest of the wall.

Mr. Green is a trustee and he fixes things around God's Church all the time. Mr. Green calls God's Church his church home too; but he doesn't live here like I do. It's easy to see he cares for the church and wants to do his part in taking care of things that need fixing.

One of my favorite days at God's Church is Thursday, the day the children's choir comes to practice their songs. It's so exciting for me as time for their choir practice draws near: I often fly to the back door, race to the front door, scurry to the piano, then out to the kitchen and back to the front door again. The children soon arrive and, being very tired, I go to my lovely warm nest in the back of the church where the carpet is turned up and listen to the children sing about God.

Oh what joy! What a heavenly sound! I feel good all over knowing how much the children like to sing about God, in God's Church, on Thursday afternoon.

Sometimes, while listening to the joyful music of the children's choir,

I close my eyes and dream my favorite dream;

about a boat.

It isn't an ordinary houseboat. It isn't an ordinary sail boat. It's an EXTRA-ordinary Mouse Boat! (You might even call it a Ship.)

I want to sail in my very own ship on beautiful Blue Lake near God's Church.

In case you haven't noticed, I love God very, very much. And, being a church mouse and all, I know what it's like to be able to live in God's house. I know people like to come to God's Church on Sunday morning and sing songs about God, and listen to the pastor talk about God, and pray to God with their eyes shut. I'm very interested in the ways of PEOPLE. I've noticed not all people pray with their eyes shut! But, being a church mouse, I know God hears prayers whether eyes are closed or open.

Back to my dream....

I remember, from reading the Mouse Translation (MT) of my Bible, Jesus was very interested in boats. Many times he came to be with his disciples when they were riding in boats and fishing in boats and doing all the things that people do in boats.

In my dream, Jesus comes to sail with me on my boat as we drift from shore to shore on beautiful Blue Lake. I know how wonderful it would be to be very, very close to him. My dream of sailing with Jesus in my very own boat brings real pleasure to me. (In case you haven't noticed, I spend a lot of time dreaming.)

Except...

My dreams are sometimes interrupted by PEOPLE. People come to God's Church to DO things, like putting on DINNERS and having SUNDAY SCHOOL classes, and YOUTH meetings, and PRAYER meetings, and more meetings like FINANCE, and MISSIONS, and WORSHIP COMMITTEE, and CHOIR PRACTICE, and FINANCE MEETINGS. (Whatever "finance" is, there it is again.) And TRUSTEE meetings...and..

Oh my!

It's hard to find time to dream at all with the meetings to attend and classes to attend, and dinners to attend. (I especially like the after dinner clean up time.) Then there is painting to do and lawns to mow and FINANCE? Well it's getting so I am so busy attending meetings and dinners and choir practice and more, I hardly have time to dream about my ship and a wonderful friendship with Jesus as we drift from shore to shore on beautiful Blue Lake not far from God's Church.

You may have noticed, I am a very happy, very warm, very lively, and yes even lovely (if I do say so myself,) church mouse.

My dream, even though I don't have much time to dream it any more, gives me something to think about when I'm not busy doing things for God's Church.

AND THEN IT HAPPENED!

You aren't going to believe this, but it really happened. It was on a sunny Sunday morning and the announcements were being read. I was in my bed in the usual place at the end of the sanctuary where the carpet is curled up. I was watching the people praying with their eyes shut. Then I heard it!

TOMORROW. IT WOULD BE NICE IF YOU ALL COULD ATTEND. WE WILL DISCUSS...STEWARDSHIP.

I stood frozen on my favorite piece of carpet. My ears were quivering. A series of loops totally out of my control appeared in my tail. My eyes filled with tears.

God's people were going to have a meeting about Steward's Ship. I didn't think I could wait until Monday.

* * *

The meeting began promptly at 8 p.m. There were only 10 people attending. I was astonished at such a small number of people attending such an important church meeting in which I, personally, had a tremendous interest. Hadn't the minister invited ALL the people to attend? Maybe, just maybe, ALL the people weren't interested in Steward's Ship. There was one thing for sure, I would be forever grateful if those 10 people could help to make my dream come true.

Jonathan Steward's Ship... I would have my very own ship to sail on lovely Blue Lake, with Jesus by my side.

This would definitely be the most important evening I had ever spent in God's Church. These 10 wonderful people were going to spend the entire meeting talking about Steward's Ship.

Suddenly I perked up my ears!

Mr. Smith was talking about the need to have more people come to the Sunday worship service. What had that to do with my ship? Mr. Green was saying something about the need to fix a hole in the church roof. My stars, couldn't anyone stay on the subject at hand?

Mrs. Jones, sitting on the edge of her chair, said, "We certainly need to encourage more people who like to sing, to join our choir." And then, Mr. Black, the chairman said...

"Maybe we should concentrate on getting to know each other and enjoying a closer personal friendship with God, and getting to know Him better and learn how to serve Him in God's Church and out of God's Church and...." (Whew, I said to myself, as I whisked perspiration from my forehead, now they're getting back to the subject at hand.) My dream ship was just the place for me to get closer to God.

AND...

I live in God's Church and spending time on my dream ship would give me opportunities to be out of God's Church on sunny days. Through God's Church people, I was about to have my dream come true.

My ears literally crossed at what I heard next.

"Of course", the Steward's Ship committee chairman was saying, "we must realize that many people here in God's Church don't really know what Steward's Ship is and it's our place to explain it to them."

I simply could not take it any more. This meeting had gotten out of hand. Of course, everyone knew what Steward's Ship was. Well, didn't they? This very meeting had been called to discuss it. Hadn't it?

"One of the best things we could do," (the committee chairman was still speaking), "would be to make sure our members and friends here at God's Church understand all the many ways there are for Christians to offer stewardship to God through the church.

They want to offer my ship to God?

I felt a lump in my little mouse throat and a warm tear slowly tumbled down my nose. But, it didn't seem to me that the chairman was talking about MY ship. It didn't seem possible, it couldn't be possible there was another kind of Steward's Ship.

Until now, I had been sitting very, very still and listening very, very closely and leaning comfortably against the leg of Mrs. Jones' chair. OFFER STEWARD'S SHIP TO GOD?

"And", the chairman was saying, "everyone in God's church is a STEWARD.

THAT DID IT!

I couldn't help myself. I jumped straight up into the air from the special place I had been listening, right beside Mrs. Jones' leg. My long grey tail...oh dear...brushed against...oh my..Mrs. Jones' leg!

And Mrs. Jones, oh my, well to put it mildly...Mrs. Jones EXCLAIMED LOUDLY!

I was startled to say the very least, and upset to say more than the very least. I headed straight to my lovely warm nest in the back of the church to recover my composure. I'm sure the entire committee on Steward's Ship and Mrs. Jones, attempted to regain their composure too.

I began to think about the events of the evening and the meeting on Steward's Ship. As soon as I felt calmer I very quietly crept back to the door of the committee room. (Not the inside of the door, mind you, but the outside.) I very carefully tucked my long grey tail beneath me. I certainly didn't want to upset anyone again. I really needed to hear more about their description of Steward's Ship.

The members of the committee had now regained their composure. I listened intently as Mr. Brown spoke. "We should tell people about all the things that are part of stewardship", he said. "Like mowing the lawn and fixing holes in the plaster, working on dinners and serving on committees such as the Worship Committee and the Education Committee.

I was amazed. Apparently there was quite a bit about their kind of Steward's Ship that I hadn't heard. I already knew about all those things Mr. Brown was speaking about. What I didn't know was that PEOPLE called the doing of those things STEWARDSHIP.

I was beginning to get a joyful feeling again. Yes I was. I was feeling joy for sure.

Mrs. Jones was saying, "We must tell God's Church people that the doing of these things helps to bring them into a closer relationship to God".

I was stunned! Yes I was. I was stunned! A closer relationship with God was exactly what I was looking for and I was sure I could find that on my own little ship, Steward's Ship, while sailing around on the lovely blue lake close by.

I began to wonder if it was possible the very thing I was hoping for could be found right here in God's Church? It could be found in my very own church home?

"And", the chairman was saying, "We need to explain to God's Church people about finance". (There was that word again, FINANCE.) What did FINANCE have to do with their stewardship for heaven's sake? I edged closer because I was determined to find out once and for all about this FINANCE thing.

We have to let the people know that the finance of the church, the people's offering of their money for God's use, is the most important part of stewardship.

MONEY??

I felt myself breathing a sigh of relief. Money was one thing a mouse doesn't have to worry about. But, as I listened, I began to realize that money and the offering of it to God's Church is part of what God expects from His people. I began to realize, with a bit of surprise, that the giving of a portion one's money to God's Church brings people into a closer relationship with God.

I began to realize something else. My dream ship hadn't been lost. In fact, it wasn't lost at all. My dream was real. I could get closer to God right here in my own church home by working and serving and helping and giving of my mousetime..my mouse abilities and mouse knowledge, especially on church mouse problems.

I knew without a doubt, that even though church mice don't have money, once God's people learned what stewardship is, they would give their time, their money and their abilities to the church. Because of their giving, God's people would have a closer relationship to God.

I felt good. I felt warm and joyful again and all happy inside,

I returned to my lovely warm nest at the back of the sanctuary and slept.

I felt safe in the knowledge that I was very, very close to God.

BACK TO THE FUTURE

Grandpa

December 7, 1941

The Unknown Of Camping

December 7, 1941

1951
(By Mary Anne Whitchurch)
Tenth Grade High School

On a cold, gray morning
when the fog had yet to rise,
the seagulls made a flutter
like a bird of paradise.

The waves were as a rose vine
coils in an arbor,
Thus began the day
Japanese bombed Pearl Harbor.

The sun had yet to rise that day,
December seven.
Dawn had just receded
to another day in heaven,

When from the sky a frightful noise
came booming from a gun.
Now in the place of clouds and sky
had come;
The Rising Sun.

Their guns were all ablaze.
From the air there came a shrieking
of bullets,
whizzing by to find their targets,
quickly streaking.

The planes upon the ground
were shattered as they stood.
For the men to take their stations,
Would, of course, have done no good.

The people who had lived at Pearl Harbor
were not spared.
Families of the fighting men

were sadly not prepared.

A couple that had risen right at dawn
to walk for pleasure,
were shattered, killed by bullets
which were made for such a measure.

A moment quickly passed,
now the air was filled with death.
Looking toward the morning sky,
only clouds were left.

The sun had risen in the east;
its bright light showed a flood
of red, red streaks
upon the ground,
now sadly stained
with blood.

The stillness in the morning air
seemed empty,
dark and chilling.
A group of planes had quickly come.
Their one intent was killing.

The second world war began.
With it came the strife
for families of the men
whose fate it was
to lose their life.

Pearl Harbor was the turning point
in nineteen forty-one.
It was to bring a mask of death
for five long years to come.

The seventh day of every month
we pause
and should remember

The Japanese bombed Pearl Harbor
on the seventh of December.
* * *

I've often wondered at the intensity of thought
of myself as a 16 year old girl
considering the awful event of Pearl Harbor.

This was written in 1951.
The event had happened only ten years earlier.
Although it seems to us in 2023
as only a point in history,
it was very real to a teen-aged girl
in those times.

The war had been over for 6 years at the time I wrote this.
It still remained fresh in the minds of our people.

The men and women who served in the war,
A few of whom are still with us today,
can never erase the images
of the horror they witnessed
during their time of service to our country.

If we cannot remember what happened
on December 7, 1941,
investigate the history books.

It must never happen again.
* * *

111

Grandpa!
My Favorite Relative

American Literature Class
(1952 10th Grade)
Mary Anne Whitchurch

My grandfather is a wonderful man. Among all of my relatives, he is my favorite. Grandpa isn't a very tall man but he makes up for it in his booming voice and proud way.

Grandpa has big, bushy eyebrows, once jet-black, which are turning steel-gray with age. I describe his eyebrows because if you ever saw him, the lasting impression of him would be his eyes.

When Grandpa is happy his eyes seem green and have a twinkle in them. But when Grandpa is unhappy, those flashing eyes are cold and gleaming. His heavy eyebrows knit together.

The thunder in his voice seems as a storm brewing and his eyebrows loom as big, dark and billowing clouds on the horizon.

Grandpa has a bald spot on the top of his head and his hair surrounds it. That rim of gray, curly hair refuses to lie down. It sticks out over his forehead.

Grandpa looks a great deal like an Indian for he has a large broad nose and high cheekbones. His ears are large and his skin is dark like an Indian.

Grandpa is usually smoking a cigar. The smell of it is quite pleasant to me, for I know when it is the first thing I smell when I get home from school; he and Grandma are visiting.

And I'm glad!

The Unknown Of Camping

By Marianne Whitchurch 10th Grade English
1952
I've loved writing since high-school.

While searching through some files today, I found this missile written by me in the tenth grade. At first glance, it looks like this is the actual paper I turned in for the assignment; so much for presentation and neatness.

(At second glance, it actually is the original paper; no corrections, teachers comments etc.) She gave me an A- for composition and a B for method.

My English teacher was a young woman just out of college. When looking back on my high school days, she comes to mind as one of my favorites. Maybe it was because I loved writing and the English Class, or maybe it was a combination of English, writing, and the teacher. Her name was *Elyse Heinecke*.

Perhaps it was because I loved everything about high school.

We may never know for sure.

As I recall, this harrowing description of *camping out*, goes back to one adventure where I woke up the next morning feeling just as described. Needless to say, camping has never been a favorite adventure of mine since that overnight incident.
She said we could write about anything we wished. This was my wish.

This idea of camping outside isn't all it's cracked up to be.
You start out on a bright, cheerful, sunny day with your spirits high and your car or truck loaded with all sorts of camping equipment, half of which you will never use. You arrive at the lake full of fresh air and sunshine and fairly pawing the earth to begin setting up your tent.
The lake is breath-takingly beautiful with its surface as smoothe as glass. The color is like blue velvet lying on a carpet of rich green grass. The first thought that runs through your childish little mind is how pretty, cool, and serene it will be in the early morning.

After you set up the battered old army tent which looks only large enough to house a tiny puppy, the sun is sinking in the golden west and you decide you'd better go and hit the sack so you can get an early start. You want to get up with the birds and catch a mess of fish for breakfast.
The next thing you know you are crawling into bed with dreams slowly drifting through your head of getting a fresh start in the morning.
Before you know it, you hear a strange singing noise and you quietly sleep on because you have a queer idea in your fogged up brain that someone is singing to

you. Suddenly you wake with a rousing start and fairly hit your head on the top of the tent. For some reason you itch all over and you can't figure out what it is.

Suddenly it dawns on you.
There are mosquitoes swarming around the tent like dive bombers and their target is you. They are as big as elephants and make about as much noise as three squadrons of planes.
Somehow you manage to get back to sleep, but you aren't quite as sure of this screwy idea of a camping trip as you once were.
The gray dawn finally comes and you crawl out of that hole called a tent with as many kinks as a pretzel and enough mosquito bites to furnish an army of people for a year.

Now to get to the beautiful little boat that you discovered last evening.
As you drag yourself down to the calm, serene lake you accidentally step in some sticky gray muck that has about as much pull as quicksand.
After you have struggled bravely with this for awhile, a light goes on in your tiny little head and you think how wonderful that feather bed at home would be.
In a short time this idea has grown on you and before long you find yourself leaving that mud with unbelievable strength.
Jumping into your shiny black car you zoom quickly for home never again to venture out on a camping trip until the next time you get a crazy idea that's what you want to do.

Musings
Of
A Homemaker

By Mary Anne Tuck
(Houghton Lake Resorter)
Houghton Lake, Michigan

1961
1962
1963
1964
1965

Musings Of A Homemaker
Index with Recipes

1961
Musings

MUSINGS
OF A
HOMEMAKER
(Anonymous)
November 16, 1961
(Houghton Lake Resorter)
Houghton Lake, Michigan

It's beyond compare;
this thrilling season, this window shopper's paradise, this wonderful
spending season when even the very thriftiest housewife has a legitimate
and commendable reason for spending her husband's money on
luxurious and useful items for "just plain giving."
The remainder of the year is consumed in budgeting and the
interminable weighing of needs against wants; with the former nearly
always overshadowing the latter in the final accounting.
Whoever it was that said, "It is more blessed to give than to receive",
must surely have included the unembellished joy of planning and
shopping for gifts for giving. Not to mention, of course, the great
personal pleasure which is involved in creating something to give to a
relative or friend as a very real part of oneself.
This also is the time when those of you who are planning to create a gift
from your own special reserve of talents, are looking for new ideas,
patterns, and recipes; exchanging your own favorites with friends and
relations in the never ending quest for "something different."
We begin to weave that wonderful web of holiday atmosphere that
entangles us in the season's festivities.
Whether you are an early shopper, or dependent upon that last minute
scurry-up trip to complete your list, you'll be enchanted with every single
moment of the hustle and bustle of the holidays.
For anyone interested in a simple pattern for crocheting mittens for your
favorite child, we'll be happy to send one to you in return for your self-
addressed, stamped envelope.

MUSINGS OF A HOMEMAKER
(Anonymous)
November 30, 1961
(Houghton Lake Resorter)
Houghton Lake, Michigan

The first day of December; tomorrow.
Impossible but true. 1961 is in its final 30 day outburst of Yuletide tradition that brings each year to its glorious end.
We've all been so involved in our fall preparations-Labor Day, the first day of school, Halloween, deer season, and Thanksgiving; the sparkling yet serene month of December is nudging November into the gone but not forgotten eternity of memories of another year.
We wonder about the commercial aspects of the Christmas season with a mounting concern lest we forget the true meaning of the anniversary of the birth of our Lord; and yet, it is a time for rejoicing in the brotherhood of man, a happy, joyful time when our hope may be rekindled by a miracle that happened over two thousand years ago.
We can all plunge into the overflowing warmth of greeting cards and gift giving, tree trimming and menu planning with the gaiety and spirit of a nation confident in the knowledge that we are applying the true meaning of the holidays to each cherished family tradition.
Since we are a nation blessed in an abundance of food; we homemakers are always looking for something new to put a sparkle into the eyes of our own very special family. We think we've found just the thing in a zippy recipe for fruit bars to enhance that holiday cup of coffee shared with friends on a cold December evening.

2 cups raisins	4 eggs
1 cup dates	3 cups sifted flour
1 cup dried apricots	1 tsp salt
1 cup diced mixed candied fruits	1/2 tsp baking pwd
1 cup chopped walnuts	1/2 tsp baking soda
1 cup butter or margarine	1 tsp cinnamon
1 1/2 cups brown sugar (packed)	1/2 tsp cloves
1/4 cup molasses	1/2 tsp allspice

2 tsp vanilla

Cover raisins, dates and apricots with boiling water and let stand 5 min. Drain, cool and chop. Combine with fruits and nuts. Cream together butter, sugar, molasses, and eggs. Combine flour with salt, baking pwd, soda and spices, blend into creamed mixture. Spread in 2 greased 10 x 15 x 1 inch pans. Bake in mod. Oven 25 to 30 min. Cool in pans. Frost with powdered sugar frosting if desired. Cut into squares. Yield 8 dozen bars.

If you'll send us your favorite holiday recipe, we'll share it with the folks!

3

MUSINGS OF A HOMEMAKER
(Anonymous)
December 7, 1961
(Houghton Lake Resorter)
Houghton Lake, Michigan

We haven't forgotten what the spiritual significance of Christmas means to the ultimate hope of the world, nor, have we forgotten to instill that meaning into the hearts and minds of our children. But, who can deny the added pleasure of a child's enchantment with the mysteries of Santa and his magnificent reindeer.

We who have passed through those portals of girl and boy land, have been warned we may never return again; but someone has overlooked our unique opportunity to relive those childhood memories through the eyes of our young ones.

They are eagerly willing to accept, without question, the time worn tale of the jolly, bewhiskered gentleman who magically covers the earth with happiness in the hours from midnight 'till dawn on Christmas Eve.

We, too, can hear those tinkling sleigh bells and see that far-off trail in the sky that can only mean Saint Nicholas is once again at his honorable profession of filling each child's heart as well as his stocking with memories to treasure throughout the years.

Among those memories, you may be assured, will remain the pleasant, tempting aroma of Mother's kitchen; kitchens of young wives the world over can never quite equal. No rival is as difficult to compete with as a memory.

So for all those young wives, we have a recipe for Raisin Cookies which we borrowed from grandma's very own recipe box. Even the novice cook may present her better half some sweets as good as he remembers Mom's.

1 1/2 cups brown sugar	2 cups flour
1/2 cup butter	1 tsp. cinnamon
2 eggs-beaten	1/2 tsp. cloves
1/2 cup sour milk	

1/2 tsp. nutmeg

1 cup raisins

Mix ingredients in order given. Drop by teaspoonfuls on cookie sheet.
Bake 10-12 minutes in 350 deg. oven.
Don't forget....just 14 shopping days left!

MUSINGS OF A HOMEMAKER
(Anonymous)
December 14, 1961
(Houghton Lake Resorter)
Houghton Lake, Michigan

It appears we might have a white Christmas after all.
It wouldn't be just right without a sparkling blanket of new fallen snow,
and let us hope we get it.
We can prepare and plan and see the season through, but without the
crowning touch to cover the brown winter coat of Nature's barren beauty,
our hearts and minds can never quite agree on the anticipated, yet
sentimental, splendor of a white Christmas.
Have you seen it in the eyes of a child upon witnessing the wonder of the
first snow of winter? Remember how grand it was to make the very first
tracks in a field of white on a frosty December morning?
We feel just a bit sympathetic toward those folks who left our winter
wonderland for the agreeably warmer climate of some of our southern
states. Of course, everyone isn't as fond of frosty windshields and cars
that have to be persuaded into frozen mobility as the "died in the wool"
Michigander who wouldn't trade it for all the warm, sunny weather the
south has to offer.
We suggest you treat yourself and your family to a snowy drive through
our scenic trails, just off the beaten path. If you enjoyed them during our
warm, summer days, then don't miss the unequaled beauty of pine trees
heavily laden with white, wonderful, glittering snow. And, if you're lucky
enough to glimpse one of our White-tail deer bounding through the
green and white of a Michigan forest in resplendent winter grandeur; you
can count yourself among the fortunate who live in this "God's Country"
of the North.
We can treat ourselves not only to the wonders of the eye, but also to the
hearty appetites so readily called upon after a day of winter sightseeing.
You'll want something quick and simple to fix for a snack. We suggest
you try making bar-b-q's from canned corned beef and canned spaghetti
sauce. (One can of meat to two cans of sauce.) Serve it hot in warmed

hamburger buns with a side dish of potato chips and a steaming cup of coffee.

You'll have some extra, so why not invite the neighbors in for the evening and regale them with your thrilling winter driving experience through our boundless north woods trails.

See you next week!

MUSINGS OF A HOMEMAKER
(Anonymous)
December 21, 1961
(Houghton Lake Resorter)
Houghton Lake, Michigan

"Santa knows we're all God's children,
that makes everything right"...
The strains of caroling and the songs of the holiday season come to us,
not only through the magic of electronics, but through the memories of
other Christmases; just as wonderful, just as sentimental, just as highly
anticipated as the one which is nearly upon us.
Eyes aglow, cheeks rosy red; we're happily weary from our bout with
Christmas shopping, tree trimming, greeting card lists and holiday party
menus. They are all a grand and glorious part of every family's
Christmas.
It's come to this down through the years; each generation has willed to
posterity, the special observances of the holidays.
The oldest tradition, handed down thousands of years, is the giving of
gifts to show our love and adoration for a tiny baby, born in a manger
because the inn was too crowded to accommodate his mother, the
blessed Mary.
The birth of the Christ Child was such an event then, now and forever.
Almost two thousand years hence, we still celebrate the occasion of His
birth with the most reverent prayers that we may offer.
The original gifts of gold, frankincense, and myrrh have blossomed into
the giving of gifts the world over, following the manner of the first
celebration.
On this Christmas Eve day, we'll have an opportunity to attend the
church of our choice to offer a prayer of thankfulness for the birth of our
Savior, whose presence on earth, centuries ago, left us with a desire for
building and living a life as near to His as is humanly possible.
With each gift given and received on Christmas morning, let us also give
and receive a silent prayer in honor of the reason for each remembrance;
the birth of a tiny child, Christ our Lord.

May you all have the most joyous Christmas, the happiest day, and the
inner peace you desire on this special occasion,
Christmas Day, the year of our Lord, 1961.

1962
Musings

MUSINGS OF A HOMEMAKER
(Anonymous)
January 4, 1962
(Houghton Lake Resorter)
Houghton Lake, Michigan

Our closets may be a little fuller,
our cupboards a little emptier;
lives are much richer for having shared the annual holidays with beloved
families and friends.
Most of us have compiled, either mentally or on paper, a properly
serious list of New Year's resolutions. By now we've destroyed said list
accurately, precisely, and completely.
Here we are right smack in the middle of winter.
Chin up folks, we can look forward to all sorts of nice things.
Next on tap being our mid-winter "shot-in-the-arm"; Tip-Up-Town
U.S.A., as only Houghton Lake can produce it with all its good natured
hi-jinks and just plain fun.
There will be unlimited ice-fishing for those of us who are partial to the
great outdoors; a nice cozy chair by the fire and a book, for those of us
who are not.
If you are a lucky homemaker who is blessed with a wonderful husband
whose only fault is, he loves to make a batch of fudge when you've just
gotten the kitchen tidied up after supper, settle down in the
aforementioned comfortable chair with the aforementioned good book,
and find him a simple recipe for creamy fudge that will help keep your
kitchen reasonably clean.
Concentrate on your book and let him enjoy his cooking.

MUSINGS OF A HOMEMAKER
(Anonymous)
February 1, 1962
(Houghton Lake Resorter)
Houghton Lake, Michigan

The high cost of living, or is it the cost of high living?

Whatever it's called, it was down during the month of December one tenth of one percent; reports the bureau of all such fascinating information.

In looking over, (or over-looking), our own report on such indispensable items as no doubt appear in the cost of living index, we find our own "cost of living" remains much the same. If we could only do away with eating, accustom ourselves to living in "really cool" homes, and trust to luck (with fingers crossed) nothing bad will happen; we could cut down on all insurance policies, immeasurably changing our cost of living.

Maybe the time of year has some bearing on the subject. At our house, as in so many homes, we're doing our annual budget search; trying to account for the reason our "cost of living"so greatly exceeds our "living costs".

Of course, the fact we've just received property tax notices, combined with the receipt of the Federal Income Tax folder, no doubt constitutes the *cause* and our seemingly flattened budgets are the *effect.*

We'll just have to continue to remind ourselves that it is a privilege to pay taxes and to live in a country where such privileges made it the greatest nation in the world.

As for this reported decrease in the cost of living during the month of December, when you pause to consider, that is remarkable in itself. Just when we've decided that the price of almost everything is going up, the cost of living comes down.

It is encouraging to we homemakers, though, who are sincerely looking for ways to cut corners. Of course, we can always be on the look-out for money saving, time saving recipes; speaking of that, here's one that will save on both.

RAISIN PUDDING
Cream 1 tblsp butter with 1/2 cup sugar. Add 1/2 cup milk. Sift together 1 cup flour, 1/2 tsp soda, 1/2 tsp nutmeg and 1/4 tsp salt. Mix all ingredients together into a smooth batter. Then add 1/2 cup raisins and 1/4 cup chopped walnuts. (Optional)
Spread in bottom of a 1 1/2 quart casserole. Pour hot sauce, (see recipe following) carefully over the top and bake 30 minutes in 375 deg. oven. Serve with milk if desired.

HOT SAUCE
Mix 1 cup brown sugar with 2 tblsp butter and 2 cups boiling water. Place over medium heat until all is dissolved.

8

MUSINGS OF A HOMEMAKER
(Anonymous)
February 8, 1962
(Houghton Lake Resorter)
Houghton Lake, Michigan

Here we are safely through another holiday,
that's right!
Hope you didn't miss it! Although it wasn't marked in red on our
calendar, the words were under the date just the same.
It read, "Ground Hog Day".
If you missed this annual, eagerly awaited, "future telling" day, then you
aren't aware that we are sadly due for six more weeks of ice and winter
weather.
According to the legend, the remaining days of winter only amount to six
weeks if the little fellow sees his shadow. But, I'm afraid no one knows
"weather" or not we will have specifically that many weeks of blowing
winds and dropping mercury. From past experience we are inclined to
think it will be more like eight, ten, or even twelve weeks.
It's only fitting that such a chilling prediction weather-wise, should be
followed by the year's only warm-hearted holiday, St. Valentine's Day.
This is the day when each and every husband and sweetheart expresses
his devotion via a lovely (or funny) card, trimmed in red hearts and a lacy
fringe. The message enclosed is strictly up to the sender.

Mom's have their own special way of presenting loved ones with a
valentine. After all, "The way to a man's heart is through his stomach".
Here's where where she shines; putting all her love into a beautiful cake
and watch husband and family glow as they realize this valentine belongs
to them and them alone.
We have a recipe this week to fulfill a valentine wish. Of course, we call
it "Sweetheart Cake".
9 egg yolks
3 tsp Baking Powder
1 1/2 cups sugar

3/4 tsp salt
3/4 cups boiling water
1 1/2 tsp. Lemon extract
2 1/2 cups sifted cake flour

Beat egg yolks until light. Add sugar gradually, then the water and continue beating. Add flour, sifted with the baking powder and salt. Beat thoroughly. Add flavoring. Bake in 3 qt mixing bowl. Frost with Seven Minute Frosting, sprinkle with tinted coconut and decorate with tinted butter frosting, using a cake decorator. Bake 50-60 min. 325 deg. Oven NOTE To tint coconut add 1 to 2 drops of vegetable coloring to 3 tblsp warm water. Add 1 cup coconut and stir until entirely colored. Dry on waxed paper.

Good Luck and Happy Valentine's Day!

MUSINGS OF A HOMEMAKER
(Anonymous)
February 15, 1962
(Houghton Lake Resorter)
Houghton Lake, Michigan

President Kennedy isn't the only one
who believes in physical fitness. You'll have to admit, he did make us all
a bit more conscious of a fact we've known all along.
A prepared nation is a fit nation; fit both physically and mentally.

From time to time, almost every one of us has given some serious, if
fleeting, thoughts to a fitness program to suit our own needs. We aren't
all as active (or inactive) as our neighbor, but we could all profit from a
daily dozen push-ups, toe touching and posture correction in general.

Now, of course, there isn't one red-blooded homemaker among us who
wouldn't be righteously indignant at any suggestion that we don't get
enough exercise in our daily routine. We will tell you, and rightly so; by
the time we've finished mopping, sweeping, cleaning, reaching, bending
and stretching through our daily chores, we've had plenty of exercise.
Not to mention keeping track of anywhere from one to a dozen active
little children.
It's true though, even such industrious ladies as we are, could benefit
from a planned, daily exercise routine.
It may be a little late for New Year's Resolutions, but maybe we could
add just one more to the bottom of the list; or better still, the top.
"I hereby resolve to touch my toes at least ten times each day, so help
me". (Because, I may need help.)
Let's give it a whirl, gals! To keep the rest of the family fit as a fiddle too,
how about a protein loaded jello salad for supper this evening.
It's simple; so you'll have time to relax after your rugged exercise.
Cottage Cheese Salad
1 pkg. Lime jello-1 cup boiling water-2 cups cottage cheese-1/4 cup salad
dressing-12 or 14 marshmallows (1/2 cup)-1 small can crushed pineapple

and juice.
Dissolve jello in boiling water. Add marshmallows. Cool. Add remaining
ingredients, stirring well.
Hint For The Week
Add a pinch of salt to jello salads and desserts.
It will improve the flavor.

MUSINGS OF A HOMEMAKER

(Anonymous)
February 22, 1962
(Houghton Lake Resorter)
Houghton Lake, Michigan

It's closing in on us!
The deadline is fast approaching and most of us haven't done anything
about it!
Of course I'm referring to the annual "battle of wits" between the tax
return and the wage earner, or his wife, which turns each and every one
of us into receipt conscious deduction hunters.
Now, in place of the usual counting of sheep to soothe our troubled
nerves, we've turned to such pleasantly obvious methods as sailing snow
white receipts over calm blue seas of very large refund checks.
If you're like most of us, you'll find yourself searching diligently for those
important papers you've tucked here and there, in the corner of a
drawer, on the top shelf of a closet, and in other well preserved hiding
places out of reach of everyone including you.
At the time, it seemed like a perfect place to store them. They would be
right where you could put your hands on them.
When the lost is finally found, with a sigh of relief we promise ourselves
next year we'll put each receipt and invoice in only one place. When
next year's tax time rolls around we'll know right where to look.

Alas; it seems I remember just such a promise to myself last year; all to
no avail. Here I am once more in the midst of the "short form" the
"long form" and the "easy to follow" instructions; I just can't seem to
remember where I put the receipt for the car license, nor even how many
dependents we had at the end of the year.
(Now you'd think I'd remember that, wouldn't you?)
We'll all struggle through somehow. By April 16th we'll be able to look
back with a smile on the hectic days of preparing tax returns and forget
all about it until next year's deadline approaches.
Somehow, through it all, we still have to have nourishment and it is up to

our ingenuity to keep the family from mealtime boredom. (They should have our job, shouldn't they girls?)

This week we've got a recipe for a delicious, light dessert.

Double Raspberry Delight

1 cup boiling water   1/2 cup canned pineapple juice   1 pkg black raspberry gelatin   1 pkg frozen raspberries   1 medium ripe banana, sliced

Pour boiling water over gelatin, stirring until dissolved..Add fruit and juice. Stir until berries are thawed and gelatin is slightly thickened...About 5 minutes. Fold in banana. Spoon into sherbet glasses..Refrigerate until firm. Top with whipped cream if desired. Serves six..NOTE Do not use frozen juice.

MUSINGS OF A HOMEMAKER
(Anonymous)
March 1, 1962
(Houghton Lake Resorter)
Houghton Lake, Michigan

As President Kennedy so aptly put it,
he has been replaced as the first man of our nation in the past week and
a half by Marine Lt. Colonel John H. Glenn.
I'm sure most of us have avidly followed the comings and goings
(especially the goings) of this red headed astronaut who has captured the
heart of a nation not only by his bravery in attempting the first American
orbital flight, but by his winning smile and obvious sincerity.

It has been said the eye of the television camera captures a person as he
really is; those of us who have been glued to a television screen by the
hour since the beginning of the last "count down" will agree this man is
just the kind of man we'd choose to represent this great country of ours.
We were allowed to travel with him in his space craft, "Friendship 7",
not only through the wonders of television and radio, but through the
thrilling description by the colonel himself as he faced the throngs of
newspaper reporters with his spectacular, and in his words, "tremendous"
story of orbital flight.
Not only this man, also the other astronauts participating in the
exploration of space by the United States of America, have caught the
imagination of a free nation in their quest for knowledge of the heavens.

It makes us proud to be citizens of a country such as this where an event
of such magnitude is aired for all to see; successful or disastrous.
It provided us with one more reason for a deep and abiding love for our
country and respect for our system of government, which is unfortunately
unique in this world in which we live.
We've profited from this system in many ways. We live well, dress well,
and best of all
eat well.

MUSINGS OF A HOMEMAKER
(Anonymous)
March 8, 1962
Houghton Lake Resorter
Houghton Lake, Michigan

As defined in the dictionary...
it's a *"sweet syrup made from certain types of Maple trees"*.
To anyone who has just put away a mouthwatering breakfast of pancakes
smothered in rich, brown, delicious Maple syrup;
the definition is sadly lacking.
We've read that less than 25% of all the Maple trees in Michigan are
tapped each year for the thin, sweet tasting sap which boils down to
Maple syrup as we know it.
If you've a Maple tree in your front yard which bears brilliantly colored
leaves each fall, then why not put it to work in early spring and enjoy the
results of your labors during the year ahead?
It's still a little early for the sap to start running, but if you think you'd
like to try it this year, you'd better begin to gather a few of the necessary
items you'll need. That will include a few spiles, a galvanized bucket or
two, and a kettle to boil the sap down.
It's an invigorating time of year to be outside for even brief periods. The
effort involved,(there is a little work to it), is completely overshadowed by
the taste treat for which you are in store.
It will take approximately five gallons of sap to make one cup of syrup.
As we said, there is a little work involved; why not make it a family
project? The kids will enjoy it!
We'd welcome any new or different recipes you've found for using the
finished product. We're especially interested in a recipe for making
Maple sugar candy. If you have one, how about sending it to us and we'll
share it with all of you? Just address your recipe to The Resorter and
we'll give you credit.
In the meantime, we have a recipe for sweet rolls for that little extra
touch to a week-day meal.
Sweet Rolls

1 cake compressed yeast in tblsp of warm water and 1 tblsp sugar. Then add 1 cup lukewarm water, also 1/2 cup shortening, melted, scant 1/2 cup sugar, 3 beaten eggs, 4 cups flour with 1/4 tsp salt. After mixing, place in refrigerator over night. Divide dough in half. Roll out to 1/4 inch thick. Cut each half like a pie until you have 16 pieces in each half. Start rolling from big end. Place on cookie sheet and let raise 2 hours. Bake at 400 deg for 15 minutes.

MUSINGS OF A HOMEMAKER
March 15, 1962
By Mary Anne Tuck
(Houghton Lake Resorter)
Houghton Lake, Michigan

We've survived!
The 1962 Ice-fishing season is on its last, slushy legs. Except for a few
resourceful last minute Bluegill fisherman, the lake has seen its last spud
and shanty for another year.
You may think we're in for a brief rest before trout season and summer
lake fishing, but you've overlooked one very important item.
Once more the unlimited supply of seasonal fun has stepped in with an
off season shot-in-the-arm; sucker spearing and smelt dipping.
Every enthusiastic sportsman who has experienced the rush of churning,
swollen stream currents or the exhilarating thud of the wily fish against
his foot as nature urges the suckers upstream to spawn, can tell you that
sucker spearing is one of the fun sports of this northern country.
Furthermore, the resulting catch is good eating for those who are skilled
in the art of preparing fish for delicious meals.
The "smelt run" of the Great Lakes waters is of equal fishing fun,
although the equipment changes from spear to net.
The time honored call from the depths of a brisk, spring night; "They're
starting to run!", will bring the netters from beach fires and coffee filled
thermos jugs to fill wash tubs and buckets with the little fish by the
hundreds.
These small fish have a flavor all their own, whether dipped in flour and
popped into a butter filled frying pan or deep fat fried with a coating of
corn meal.
The grand outdoor life of our beloved north country has provided us
once more with a healthy pastime to entice the sportsman to our
bountiful woods and waters.
We'd appreciate any recipes or directions from you homemakers for
canning suckers. We've been told they are as tasty as salmon when
properly canned.

MUSINGS OF A HOMEMAKER
By Mary Anne Tuck
March 22, 1962
(Houghton Lake Resorter)
Houghton Lake, Michigan

The Vernal Equinox

A weather condition concerning the time of year when the center of the sun crosses the celestial equator and day and night are of equal length all over the earth...

That's the way the dictionary explains it, but we call it "Spring".
That one word, complete with all its pleasant connotations, is enough to make us forget about the four feet of snow lurking on our front lawns; remembering instead the bright green shoots of Tulips and Daffodils which will soon be pushing through the earth to confirm the date on the calendar.

March 20, according to the fine print, is *"the first day of spring"*.
It began Tuesday at 9:30 p.m.

It happens to all of us every year about this time. The snow covered fields and highways are beginning to wear a little thin on our nerves. We've had our plans changed once too often by "old man winter" to be ready to welcome even one more snowflake.

The annual occasion for residents of this area, *"watching the ice go out"*, is soon to be upon us. Surely even the most avid followers of the ice fishing cult have had their fill of the frosty sport for this season.

As usual, the blues affecting most of us during late March and early April are but a necessary forerunner to a most enjoyable illness we fondly refer to as *"spring fever"*.

No doubt we are due for at least one more blizzard, as is our customary fate each year in late March. It doesn't keep us from anticipating, with an eagerness too often left dormant trough the dreary winter months, the promised *"coming of spring"*.

We have another recipe to share with you this week; sent to us by a reader of The Resorter. You might also guess by the name of the sender, that this homemaker is well know to the writer of this column. Our

recipe was given to us by Mrs. Orin Tuck of the Heights, Houghton
Lake..and she calls her recipe;

Spice Crumb Cake

2 cups cake flour   1 tsp soda...1 cup sugar...1 1/2 tsp. Cinnamon...1 tsp
cloves...1/4 tsp allspice...1/4 tsp salt...1/2 cup shortening ...1 egg...2 tblsp
molasses...1 cup sour milk or buttermilk ... Sift and measure flour...Sift
three times including dry ingredients.   Cut in shortening as for pie until
mixture is very fine. Add molasses and egg...Blend well. Add milk and
beat till mix is very smooth. Turn out into well greased loaf tin.

Topping

Take two tblsp melted butter and spread over batter. Take 1 tblsp flour,
4 tblsp sugar and 1/2 tsp cinnamon. Mix together and sprinkle over top
before putting in oven. Bake at 350 to 375 deg 45-50 minutes..No
frosting is needed.

MUSINGS OF A HOMEMAKER
By Mary Anne Tuck
March 29, 1962
(Houghton Lake Resorter)
Houghton Lake, Michigan

We've had day after day of beautiful, sunny, invigorating weather;

the snow is disappearing before our eyes. The sap is running freely and the kids are no longer wearing those bulky snow clothes to school.

Get out the mops ladies. It's spring cleaning time again!
There are walls to paint, woodwork to wash and cupboards to clean.
There are ovens to scrape, refrigerators to defrost and closets to air.
The list is endless and your energy had better be too.
With all your other chores, including cooking, chauffeuring,
bookkeeping and baby-tending; now you can take on the additional,
semi-annual task of "all 'round maid".

You'll no doubt wind up with housemaid's knee, traveling muscle cramps and an aching back; your home will be ready with a fresh new face for your summertime enjoyment.
It's really a pleasure to greet each new day with the sun streaming in through the kitchen windows and the promise of spring just around the corner.
As you can see, this writer has come down with an extreme case of spring fever; the prognosis is that it will become increasingly more severe through the months of April and May.
We had a pleasant surprise in the mail this week; receiving several new recipes from southern readers via our "feminine counterpart to the boss", Mrs. Alice Hamp.
They included this recipe from a subscriber in Gulfport, Mississippi, Mrs. Sybil McEniry. It's called;
Jam Cake
1 cup butter...1 cup sugar...3 eggs...1 cup strawberry jam...1/2 cup sour

milk...1 tsp soda...1 tsp. Cinnamon...1/2 tsp cloves...1/2 tsp allspice...1/2 tsp nutmeg...2 cups flour

Cream together butter and sugar. Add eggs one at a time, beat well. Add soda to milk and stir in remaining ingredients. (May need 2 tblsp more flour) Bake in 350 deg oven; fill with raisin filling and frost with satin (brown sugar) icing.

Hats off to Mrs. McEniry!

MUSINGS OF A HOMEMAKER
By Mary Anne Tuck
April 5, 1962
(Houghton Lake Resorter)
Houghton Lake, Michigan

In a few weeks time,
we will once again have the opportunity to exercise our constitutional
rights by voting on a most important issue; whether or not to have an
additional millage on our property taxes for use of our schools.
This issue, having been voted upon several times in previous months, has
left our community "buzzing" with discussion and activity in an effort to
ascertain the necessity of such an addition.
A citizen's committee has been formed to investigate the need, and
several civic-minded citizens have voiced their views via "letters to the
editor" of the Resorter.
Each of us, homemaker and breadwinner, has an obligation to probe
deeply this unfortunate situation that has split the viewpoints of a
community so forcefully on such a vital matter of concern.
The outcome of the approaching vote is of such important consequence
that we cannot and must not approach it armed only with "half-truths"
and "hearsay" gained from well meaning friends and neighbors who
unfortunately are in no better position to judge without facts, than we are.
We have been afforded an opportunity to attend school board meetings,
read factual reports in the paper, and talk with any or all of the members
of the committee which has made a thorough study of the situation.
We each must enter the voting booth in June, armed with the "straight
dope", so we may express our decisions via the ballot box.
The right of secret ballot is never more precious, the burden of truth
never more personal than when it concerns the future of our children
and grandchildren.
We must guard their rights to education as closely as we supervise their
health and happiness.

To improve their dispositions as well as their diets, we'd like to share

with you this recipe sent us by Mrs. June Waggaman, from Kokomo,
Indiana. It's called
"Cherry Supreme"
1. Melt 1 stick butter
Pour over 2 cups graham cracker crumbs (30 crackers)
Bake 10 minutes at 350 deg...cool.
2. Mix 1 large pkg. Cream cheese (real soft), 1 cup sugar, 1 tsp vanilla.
Pour over crumbs.
3. Add 1 cup chopped nuts.
4. Add 1/2 point whipped cream
5. Add 1 large can cherry pie filling on top. Put in oblong pan
Serves 12

MUSINGS OF A HOMEMAKER
By Mary Anne Tuck
April 19, 1962
(Houghton Lake Resorter)
Houghton Lake, Michigan

Last week, April 8 to 14, was National Library week.

We were reminded of its observance on television, radio, in newspapers
and magazines.
We may or may not have given the occasion a fleeting thought; more
than likely we classified it as just another quirk of our American society
which has produced other weeks, among which "National Hot Dog
Week", "National Pickle Week", and "National Onion Week" might pass
unnoticed.
It's an unhappy fact that 25 million Americans have no public library
service.
If this year's annual "National Library Week" did nothing more than
remind us of our obligation to the children, to encourage them to read,
this would be a monumental accomplishment; worthy of some
consideration.
Although our community, unfortunately boasts no public library, we can
transport our children into a fantastic, unexplored world of knowledge
and adventure simply by placing in their eager hands the key to open the
magical door to the wonderful world of books. It is true our school
library is available for book lending to adults.
The required reading of the classroom is not only necessary to the
ultimate educational requirements of our times, it is an unavoidable
introduction to the wonders of the printed word.
Lest we forget the importance of make believe in the development of a
growing mind, search your own memory for the impression left upon it
by the tales of "Beautiful Joe" or Black Beauty"; the Bobbsey Twins" or
the delightful book of fairy tales by the brothers Grimm.
Read to your children. Let them read to you. Let them see you enjoying
the comfort of a good book so they may realize the ageless pastime.

Introduce them to reading!

Our recipe for this week was sent to us by a North Shore reader who prefers to remain anonymous. Her recipes, however, will help you to utilize that delicious Maple syrup we all love this time of year.

Maple Surprise

1 cup rice...2 cups boiling water...1 cup cream (heavy)...3/4 cup Maple syrup or 1 cup Maple sugar.

Cook rice in boiling water until tender. Drain and let cold water run through it. Beat cream and add syrup gradually. When cream begins to thicken, fold in rice. Put in cold place. If Maple sugar is used instead, it should be finely shaved and sprinkled over the whipped cream piled over the rice.

MUSINGS OF A HOMEMAKER
By Mary Anne Tuck
April 26, 1962
(Houghton Lake Resorter)
Houghton Lake, Michigan

It seems like September.

Is there one among you who could fail to detect the fresh, invigorating
aroma which comes with early spring?
We have all the symptoms of fall; grass mostly brown, forest floor has a
carpet of dry, crackling leaves, trees are barren of color.

A closer look will reveal a hint of life which cannot be denied. Tender,
green shoots are being gently persuaded to blossom under the warm rays
of bright spring sunshine.
Only spring, youngest of the four seasons, has the power to unfold the
urgency of life to the trees, the flowers and the heart of all mankind.
Show me a person who can deny the miracle of spring and I'll show you
a person who has forgotten the joy of living.
Welcoming each new day as it dawns is an art worthy of rediscovery if the
wonder of springtime has been lost to you.
We sometimes become so involved in our own daily problems, the
troubles of the world, the weight of family responsibilities; we forget the
presence of our five senses.
To hear, to see, to smell, to touch, and to taste; five common words
describing our God given abilities to enjoy life. Mistreating any one of
them by not using them to their fullest is to mistreat nature herself.
So look up! Live each day to its fullest and drink in this springtime
beauty that's all around us.
In this vast northland of endless woods and waters, we who are fortunate
enough to call it home are the envy of city-bound folks whose equally
wondrous world is not as green, clean, or spacious as our own.
Lest we forget our good fortune, we need only to remind ourselves by a
brisk walk through the woods, a picnic by the wayside, or a refreshing trip

across the lake.
We live in this country and love it!
Springtime "Up North" is a treasure of delight to young and old alike.
Recipe Of The Week
Our recipe this week was given to us by Mrs. Clare Helms of Houghton
Lake. It's called..
Spaghetti Western Style
Lightly brown in 1/4 cup drippings, 1 clove garlic, minced..1/4 cup
chopped onion, 1 green pepper..chopped. Add 1/2 pound ground beef.
Stir until meat loses color. Add 2 cans tomato sauce, 1 cup water, 1
bouillon cube, 2 tsp Worcestershire, 1 1/2 tsp salt. Blend well, cover,
simmer 40 minutes. Add 1/2 cup grated American cheese, 1/2 cup sliced
stuffed olives. Mix well. Serve hot over spaghetti (8 oz pkg)

MUSINGS OF A HOMEMAKER
By Mary Anne Tuck
May 3, 1962
(Houghton Lake Resorter)
Houghton Lake, Michigan

It's food for thought...
A museum of historical value to grace the grounds of the "Old Stone
School".
What better use could be found for the old "halls of learning" so well
remembered by many Houghton Lake alumnus, than to fill it with
remnants of years gone by for the enjoyment of many in years to come.

The relics of the lumbering days hold precious memories for those hard
working lumber-jack pioneers who have spent their lives building and
homesteading this vast area of lakes and timber.

Time was, we've heard, when land surrounding Houghton Lake was
valued at $12 per acre. Many are the would be investors who wish their
foresight had included a vision of things to come in the development of
the largest resort area in the entire state of Michigan.
Our area boasts so many natural attractions for the visitor, the vacationer,
the resident; a museum with a historic atmosphere could only serve as a
romantic link with the past for this picturesque countryside in which we
live.
On the practical side, we who make our living from the tourist trade must
readily admit a museum of this proposed nature could easily serve as a
trade attraction to the scene of our labors.
We have a unique opportunity to make our living in a land alive with
historical interest as well as a setting for attractions of nature.
A peek into the attic or the corner of the basement might reveal a
glimpse into a by-gone era of adventure and enchantment; a fascination
for all to view in a museum; now being designated by those civic minded
parties who created the idea of a museum for the "Old Stone School".

In answer to our quest for knowledge in the manner of canning suckers; we got a reply from F.T. Swarthout of Island Lodge, Houghton Lake. For those of you who are interested in the recipe, we'll be glad to send it to you upon your request. Our recipe for this week is the second from Mrs. Jane Waggaman, Kokomo, Indiana.

Spinach Casserole

2 pkg chopped spinach...1 carton sour cream...1 pkg onion soup mix...1 cup bread crumbs. Mix together after spinach has been cooked and drained. Grate cheddar cheese on top and more buttered bread crumbs. Bake at 350 deg for 25 minutes.

MUSINGS OF A HOMEMAKER
By Mary Anne Tuck
May 10, 1962
(Houghton Lake Resorter)
Houghton Lake, Michigan

To Mom...

A card, a gift, a bouquet..no tribute can adequately repay the wonderful
woman to whom we dedicate this coming Sunday,
May 13, "Mother's Day".

She gives us birth, love and gentle guidance; gifts which none but a
Mother's love can bestow. The love for her children is comparable to no
other.

It's only fitting she should have a day of her own on which honoring her,
and only her, is a nation-wide privilege.

Mother is a jewel of many facets; instinctively possessive with her infant
child. As it grows in the warmth of her love, she urgently encourages
independence from her; comforting the child through growing pains, and
chiding the young one into believing that life really isn't so bad.

Their hurts are more painful than her own, their triumphs her delight;
their love is her treasure and success in life is her success also.

She is many things to many people; counselor, guide, and confidante, but
always to us, "Mother".

"A face only a Mother could love" has more meaning than the obvious
comic interpretation. Never in our lives will we be loved as we are loved
by our Mother. The bond between Mother and child is one seldom
broken. Whether the age is one or fifty-one, Mother remains the
foremost person in life and after death, in memory.

Whether she is tall or short, plump or thin, silver-haired or dark, she's
"Mom" and because of her we are living, loving, and honoring her on her
own "Mother's Day".

Recipe of the Week

Our recipe this week was given me by my Mother, Mrs. Thomas

Whitchurch of Houghton Lake. It's delicious and different; sure to tantalize the appetites of those precious loved ones of yours. To fill your cookie jar, how about trying these?

Butterscotch Grahams

2 cups brown sugar   1 cup shortening (scant)   2 eggs, beaten   2 cups flour   1 cup graham flour (unsifted)   1 cup raisins   1 tsp vanilla   1/2 tsp salt   1 tsp soda   1 tsp baking powder

Cream sugar and shortening, add eggs, mix well. Sift together flour, salt, soda, and baking powder. Gradually stir into mixture, mix well. Add Raisins. Add vanilla Add graham flour. Mix well and drop by teaspoon on greased baking sheet. Bake at 350 deg for 12-15 minutes.

MUSINGS OF A HOMEMAKER
By Mary Anne Tuck
May 24, 1962
(Houghton Lake Resorter)
Houghton Lake, Michigan

Have you ever searched for the peaceful solitude of early morning?

No matter what your waking hour may be, a brief interlude of quiet
meditation is a welcome moment at the dawn of a new day.

The house is quiet; a condition which ceases to exist when the children
awake. The problems that weighed heavily in yesterday's light are not
nearly as impressive as they seemed. You have a new day ahead; clean,
fresh, untouched by troubles and cares.

The birds seem to sing more sweetly, the sun shines more brightly and
even the grass is aglow with a blanket of dew.
Have you ever noticed the quiet indifference of the outside world at this
hour? Before another hour passes, as if by some pre-planned signal, the
world begins to awake.
Yet, were it not for the certain knowledge of it, one could almost imagine
a complete aloneness in a world of sunshine, singing birds,and a
delightful stillness intended for pleasant thoughts and moments of utter
relaxation.

Summer days are nearly upon us. A drive through the woods displays a
bower of wild cherry blossoms in bride-like veils of white, set off by the
vibrant greens of new leaves and ferns.
Lilacs are waiting to burst forth in muted shades of violet with a fragrance
equal to the most expensive perfumes.
It seems to this writer, although other states may have warmer year
around climates, our spring and summer seasons are all the more
stimulating because of the extreme change; an awakening after months of

crisp, winter weather.
Let's welcome this heavenly Michigan spring!

Recipe For The Week
Pineapple and Cream Cheese Salad
6 slices canned pineapple 1 cup cream cheese Purple grape juice
French dressing Lettuce Leaves
Work enough grape juice into the cream cheese to soften it so that it can
be made into balls using your hands or butter paddles. Place a slice of
pineapple on a lettuce leaf, put a cheese ball on top and pour grape juice
and french dressing over all.

MUSINGS OF A HOMEMAKER
By Mary Anne Tuck
May 31, 1962
(Houghton Lake Resorter)
Houghton Lake, Michigan

Another summer beginning...
another school term ending.
With mixed emotions another graduating class is leaving the sheltered
and familiar halls of learning to venture forth into a waiting world.

To some, the journey is welcome, to others, a hesitant, faltering step into
an unknown, unfamiliar very large world.
Whatever the emotion, the path is a memorable one to those who have
made their way along the road to the future. It is hopefully long,
sometimes narrow, but always a winding avenue; complete with side trips
to higher education, marriage, family,and success in the chosen keys to
life's journey.
Ahead lie many crossroads; some to be traveled in the right direction
while others may take them to a detour, only to help gain the insight
needed to understand complicated routes to individual happiness and
fulfillment.

Remembering a promise to beloved school mates; "our class will be
different...we'll stay in touch..we won't forget"..indeed, those friendships
of high school days are never forgotten.
Names may slip from memory, faces may fade into shadows; precious
memories of young friends and comrades serve as a lifetime guide for
new and lasting friendships in years to come.
Memories of future alumni of the class of 1962 will include caps and
gowns, diplomas, and graduation day.
There will be pleasant recollections from
Houghton Lake High School.
One step...and then another!
Recipe of the Week

Rice A La Creole
1 cup chopped boiled ham...1 onion...1 cup boiled rice...1 can
tomatoes...2 cups fine soft crumbs...2 tblsp butter or other fat...Celery
salt...Pepper and salt
Mix ingredients in the order given. Bake in a greased casserole for 1/2
hour 360 deg...This dish makes a good one-dish meal.

MUSINGS OF A HOMEMAKER

By Mary Anne Tuck
June 7, 1962
(Houghton Lake Resorter)
Houghton Lake, Michigan

June 11, 1859-Gold discovered in Nevada.
June 16, 1897-Alaska Gold Rush Begins

Every Year-June is the month of brides.

It is a time when many an altar bound beauty finds a "band-of-gold" at
the culmination of a romantic discovery of her own; the beginning of a
new life for herself and some lucky fellow.
Before the trip to the altar, our modern day brides are involved in plans
and parties to overwhelm even the most active person; but with marriage
in mind a girl gains strength for such activities to be faced in the weeks
before the wedding.
She'll be securing bridesmaids, gowns, and color schemes; minister,
church and floral arrangements. There will be invitations and a never
ending list of traditional trimmings.
In the midst of this, she's caught up in a flurry of "showers, fittings and
appointments".
Through it all the bride-to-be remains calm, cool, and collected; after all,
she's realizing the dreams of her young girl-hood.
With the man she loves, an entire lifetime stretches ahead; planning a
home, a family, love and happiness in the years to come.
Since June is the traditional month of brides, it naturally precedes the
month of anniversaries. Romantic memories and treasured moments are
now in the making.
June, croon, spoon..a beautiful wedding...a bride in clouds of white;
honeymoon; tradition, ritual...
treasured memories ahead.

MUSINGS OF A HOMEMAKER
By Mary Anne Tuck
June 14, 1962
(Houghton Lake Resorter)
Houghton Lake, Michigan

A boy is wonderful...
A college man is interesting...a husband is nice...
But "Dad" is indispensable!
We love him, respect him, need him; on the third Sunday in June, we
honor him on a special "Father's Day".

Daughters adore him, sons imitate him, wives, (although they may try to
deny it), can't get along without him.
He's a tower of strength to his children, a shoulder to lean on to his wife,
provider, counselor, guide; an invaluable influence on the stability of his
family.
Dad has often been cast in the role of a comic character in various works
of fiction; the bill paying father of the bride, the responsibility shirking
disciplinarian of the children, and the henpecked husband of an
overbearing wife.
To be honest with ourselves, we must agree that somewhere in this world
there may exist such a Dad; each of us knows that he isn't our "Dad";
except perhaps for the bill paying part.
(Any Dad can tell you there is no comic aspect to the bill paying
privilege.)
It's a father's prerogative (and we respect him for it) to believe there is no
other man's son good enough to marry "his" daughter. By the same
token, a man's son deserves only the very best wife the world has to offer.
Dad is proud of his children's success in a typically masculine silence of
approval; for after all, the children are his link with the future.
They are his mark in centuries to come; his legacy to the world.
No matter the age of your Dad this Father's day, you'll remember him as
the strength of your childhood and the pattern for your adulthood. His
knowledge and wisdom on innumerable subjects has helped you to be

the person you are.

We couldn't love him more than we already do; we couldn't have more respect for any person in our life-time. We can take this one special day to really let Dad know that we regard him as a very wonderful part of our lives.

We give a very special greeting to our "Dad" on this Father's Day June 17, 1962.

Recipe For The Week

Pineapple Butterscotch Upside Down Cake

1 cup sugar 1/2 cup shortening 3/4 cup cold water 2 eggs 2 cups flour 1/2 tsp salt 3 tsp baking powder 1 tsp vanilla

Cream shortening and sugar; add beaten egg yolks. Add alternately liquid and dry ingredients. Add vanilla and mix. Fold in beaten egg whites. Grease 8 x 12 pan with butter and line pan with 1 cup brown sugar. Dot with butter. Place slices of pineapple over sugar in bottom of pan and place cherry in center of each slice. Pour batter over this and bake 50 minutes at 350 deg. Cool and turn upside down. Serve warm

MUSINGS OF A HOMEMAKER
By Mary Anne Tuck
June 21, 1962
(Houghton Lake Resorter)
Houghton Lake, Michigan

It's haying time..

Wafting a heavenly aroma which only a field of new mown hay gives forth.
For the farmer, it's a busy time, back breaking, sun-up until sun-down, labor of necessity; "make hay while the sun shines" is more than a saying.
It's a way of life.
The industrious resort owners are in the midst of their "busy time" too.
By now, they've painted and caulked, re-screened, rearranged and revitalized their places of business for the "62" tourist season.
Meanwhile, "back in the city" folks are scanning maps and marking (we hope) the most direct route to our "fan-tabulous" resort area..
City schools should, by now, be finished for the year; with the closing comes the main vacation force to our Northern areas.
At times, we find ourselves a bit envious of the carefree tourists visiting our shores each year; the "devil-may-care" fisherman, the lovely, bronzed bathing beauty, and the Sunday drivers..(On week days.)
At one time or another, each of us has complained (just a little) about the unfortunate quirk of circumstances which requires we "year around residents" of vacationland to work so diligently while all around us people are relaxing in leisure.
On the other hand, we realize not many are so fortunate as to be able to work in such a pleasant atmosphere; beautiful lake breezes, cool evenings in which to re-vitalize for another working day.
If you live in this great north country and aren't enjoying it, at least you are unhappy in pleasant surroundings.
If you live here and love it, (as most of us do) you are twice blessed and many times rewarded.
Recipe For The Week

Ginger Ale Salad
This recipe was given us by a Perrysburg ,Ohio reader
Mrs. E. H. Adams.
1 package lemon jello
1/2 cup boiling water...mix well
Add 1 1/2 cups cold gingerale and let stand until almost firm. Then add
1/3 cups apples
1/3 cup pineapple
1/3 cup nuts.
If desired, celery can be added. Chill and serve.
We'd like to share your favorite recipe with our readers. Just send it to
the Resorter and we'll print it for you.

MUSINGS OF A HOMEMAKER
By Mary Anne Tuck
June 28, 1962
(Houghton Lake Resorter)
Houghton Lake, Michigan

The peak of the strawberry season has passed.
(And it seems like only yesterday Jingle Bells was number one on the hit parade.)
Whether you purchased yours from the local vendor, or practiced a bit of do-it-yourself magic on the strawberry patch, you are already anticipating a luscious mid-winter shortcake; the labor you recently endured will seem like just another moment of summertime fun.

For some unknown reason, there has remained, through generation after generation, a home-maker's pride in the not so glamorous task of canning and preserving food for the winter months.
A feeling of achievement and loving care goes into each jar; along with strawberries, peaches, pears or whatever the seasonal harvest may bring. The same feeling goes into a cake, a pie, or a batch of homemade bread. It takes a hungry family only minutes to dispose of a day's labors; but the highest compliment you can pay a homemaker is to completely dispose of her appetizing meals before her very eyes.

When someone asks her, "And, what do you do for a living", she'll more often than not reply, "Oh, I'm just a housewife." Just..indeed! There is no task more rewarding than her's.
Through the hands of a homemaker pass the life of a nation.
She is the "first-aid, the life assurance, the peace maker, and the foundation" of every home in the world.

We've heard it said, "it's a man's world". We're a little inclined to agree. However, it's the "homemakers" who make it the most comfortable "man's world" he'll ever hope to find.
Recipe Of The Week

Strawberry Cake
Time 30-40 minutes   Temp. 325 deg
2 egg yolks
5 tblsp cold water
3/4 cup sugar
1 tblsp lemon juice
2 tsp baking powder
1 1/3 cups sifted cake flour
1/4 tsp salt
2 egg whites

Beat the egg yolks until light. Add the water, then the sugar, gradually
and continue beating. Add lemon juice. Add sifted dry ingredients
gradually to first mix. Fold in the stiffly beaten egg whites. Pour into a
torte pan with inverted bottom. Grease bottom only. When cake is cool
cut from sides with spatula. Set pan on a tall glass, and slide the rim
down. Remove inset carefully, and fill cavity in cake with sweetened
crushed strawberries and decorate with whipped cream.

MUSINGS OF A HOMEMAKER
By Mary Anne Tuck
July 12, 1962
(Houghton Lake Resorter)
Houghton Lake, Michigan

Seventeen years ago today,
the city of Berlin, Germany was zoned

At the time of the zoning, not many could imagine the plight that would
face the citizens of that foreign city today.

On July 16, 1945 this country set off in Mexico, one of the largest bomb
tests any country had ever seen. The test was so high that an enormous
effect could be seen by the naked eye 800 miles away on the Hawaiian
Islands.
The test was on the atomic bomb.

The far reaching effects of any act committed by one or a group of
responsible individuals is seldom apparent at the moment.
Remembering a line; "any good that I may do, let me do it now, for I will
pass this way but once."
It isn't only the events of the world which should give us concern, but
even more, the far reaching effects of neighbor to neighbor, brother to
brother, friend to friend.
No matter how small the act, the significance is in the deed. A friendly
gesture, a kind word, a measure of friendship, may be all that is needed
in a world of unrest and indecision.

Towns, states, nations; the world is made up of individuals most of whom
are trying to understand the rights and beliefs of one another.
Many of us have adopted the attitude of not concerning ourselves with
the affairs of the world. Most of us feel that since we are powerless to
change anything, we may as well leave the problems to the politicians; the
heads of state whose job it is to be concerned with such matters.

However, we are concerned with our own area. We can do something about our own neighborhoods, our own back yard, and our own families. We can profit by remembering the plight of areas who have turned their backs on the sanctity of home and family; losing pride in their communities.

We can develop our community to measure up to the basic beginning provided by Mother Nature; untouched forests, bountiful lakes, and unlimited opportunity.

It really is better to light one candle, than to curse the darkness.

Recipe For The Week

Brownie Cookies

1/2 cup shortening

1/2 cup granulated sugar

1/4 cup brown sugar

1 egg

1/2 tsp salt

1/2 tsp soda

1 tsp vanilla

1 (1 oz) square unsweetened chocolate, melted)

2 tblsp milk

1 cup sifted flour

1/2 cup chopped walnuts

Cream together shortening and sugars, egg and vanilla till light and fluffy. Stir in chocolate and milk. Sift together dry ingredients. Stir into creamed mix, blending well. Add nuts. Drop by rounded tsp 2" apart on greased cookie sheet Bake at 350 deg 10-12 minutes or until done. Cool Slightly..Remove from pan. Makes 2 dozen

We would still like to share your favorite recipe. Please send it to us in care of the Resorter Office and we'll pass it on to our readers!

MUSINGS OF A HOMEMAKER
By Mary Anne Tuck
July 19, 1962
(Houghton Lake Resorter)
Houghton Lake, Michigan

Here we are in the midst of the "let's eat outside" season!

It's a hearty, appetizing, family time for kids from 6 to 60.
Just mention bar-b-q's or grilled steaks; you'll find Dad with eyes aglow
and seasoning in hand to take over at least this one chore from Mom.
For him, the grill must be at a precise measure above the coals, the steak
of proper quality and thickness; heaven help the little woman who offers
a casual suggestion. That will be labeled as infringing on his outdoor
culinary domain.
Strangely, a man who enjoys this outdoor cookery is usually quite adept
at presenting a pleasing and palatable taste treat for family and friends.

It's relaxing for him in fanciful comparison to his usual work-a-day
routine; his approach is precise and scientific. He's in command and he
enjoys every minute of it.
Let's not overlook the fact that Mom rather enjoys Dad's taking over in
the grilling department too.

The kids are wild about grassy carpets which soak up spilled milk. And
there's a noticeable lack of parental reminders such as; "don't slouch,
don't talk so much, and for heaven's sake haven't you eaten enough?"

Outdoor eating is fun and the entire family welcomes the change of
routine and the cooling breeze after a warm day engaged in summertime
tasks.
These are the months when hot dogs, hamburgers, and potato salad
become household words. Cold fried chicken, ham and iced tea are old
standbys which we've come to depend upon. We never tire of them as
long as the picnic table beckons and the family awaits the enjoyment of
the "outdoor eating season".

Recipe Of The Week

We were very pleased to receive a note and a recipe from Mrs. Clare Keith, 516 Brandon Street, Owosso. She reads our column and wants to share one of her favorites with us. It's called;

Chicken Luncheon

1-4 pound chicken-cooked-remove bones

2 cups fresh bread crumbs

1 cup cooked rice

1 1/2 tsp salt

2/3 cup broth

4 eggs

Mix above ingredients together.

Gravy

1/4 cup butter

1 small can mushrooms

1/4 cup flour

1/4 cup cream

1 pint chicken broth

Add pimento for color 1 tsp lemon juice

After gravy is cooked, mix with the chicken mixture and bake slowly for 1 1/4 hours

We'd like to share your recipe with our readers, too. Send it to us in care of The Resorter.

MUSINGS OF A HOMEMAKER
By Mary Anne Tuck
July 26, 1962
(Houghton Lake Resorter)
Houghton Lake, Michigan

A day to go down in communications history!

What a thrill to be afforded an opportunity to watch television live,
continent to continent, by a signal bounced off a battery satellite orbiting
the earth!
Was it only ten or fifteen years ago an antenna on top of a house was
considered the unusual rather than common?

Now, the possibility of "round-the-clock', inter-continental television
reception is a near certainty within the next four years.
It is difficult to encompass the fact, during a seemingly short span of time,
that such words as rocket, launch pad, astronauts and "AOK" have
become a small vocabulary of household words for kids from 5 to 85.

It hasn't taken long to advance from standard gear shifts to automatic
drives, from narrow roads to four lane expressways, and from Wilbur
and Orville to "707's". Developments have triggered a phenomenal
"rise" from highways to skyways.
We don't have to exert much effort to perform any given task from the
kitchen to the dairy bar, from the washing machine to the dry cleaners;
even in relaxation the "working fun" has been eliminated.
We have automatic toasters that don't even require the gentlest push to
down the bread for toasting. Our dairy farms have automatic milking
machines, our washers do everything but insert the dirty clothes, and the
dry cleaners require only a call for pick-up and delivery. (Or do it
yourself with the flip of a coin.)
Bowling alleys have replaced the energetic pin-boy with automatic pin-
setters, and in some of the big league ball parks the pitcher gets a ride to
the mound in the latest model car.

It's an age of automation, communication, and the sky is no longer the limit.

We've seen live through inter-continental television, reindeer in Lapland being taken to their summer grazing grounds by helicopter.

What next?

Recipe For The Day

Spaceman Peanut Butter Buns

(For little Astronauts)

1 medium fully ripe banana

1/2 cup peanut butter

1 tblsp lemon juice

Parkerhouse rolls or hamburger buns

Mash banana. Add peanut butter and lemon juice. Spread on buttered rolls. Makes one cup of filling. Applesauce variation..Use 1/2 cup applesauce instead of banana and omit the lemon juice.

MUSINGS OF A HOMEMAKER
By Mary Anne Tuck
August 2, 1962
(Houghton Lake Resorter)
Houghton Lake, Michigan

Summer is having its final fling.

It's now or never for the vacationer, the trout fisherman and the "less than eager" scholar who clings to August with fervent hope.

Past years have proven this month to be the hottest weather, the sunniest days and the happiest hours for warm weather advocates the nation over. For those born in this late summer month, the birth-stone is Sardonix or Peridot; a lovely green gem, symbolic of a relaxing summer day.

We're preparing for a change of seasons. Homemakers are busily canning and preserving garden fresh fruits and vegetables for cold winter months.
It's been a warm and pleasant, rather busy summer. Area residents are anticipating a restful "after Labor Day" Indian Summer.
Although it seems a bit premature, businesses are beginning to stock and display a line of fall and winter clothing with clearance sales on swim suits, sandals, and play clothes in evidence in store after store.
Moms are making mental notes about school time wardrobes for growing youngsters. New college freshman may be entertaining doubts about the long awaited time for leaving home and getting out on their own.

It's been such a short time since New Year's Day; Memorial Day was only a few weeks ago, or so it seems. Labor Day is right around the proverbial corner.
August, the eighth month, the turning point; seven months have fled and four remain.
Let's enjoy the next thirty-one days to the hilt; we'll welcome September, fall, school days and vacation's end with open hearts, open minds, and open arms.

MUSINGS OF A HOMEMAKER
By Mary Anne Tuck
August 9, 1962
(Houghton Lake Resorter)
Houghton Lake, Michigan

Michigan is the state most likely to claim the title of the "half-way" point in the growth of our nation.

In 1837 Michigan became the 26th territory to be accepted for statehood. She has adopted children from nearly every sister state in the union; her shores are visited annually by thousands of adventuresome vacationers; seeking rest, relaxation and the secret of self satisfied Michiganders who, for the most part, would just as soon spend their own vacations right around home.

In our mid-northern county we've recently become contented shareholders to a modern and convenient boundary to boundary expressway.
The reports vary; it will bring business to our area, it will bring sight-seeing vacationers, it will bring notoriety, fame, and (we hope) fortune.

Michigan is leading the field in highway building, car manufacturing, and the furniture industry.
The state of Texas has no lead on our vast timberland of woods and waters. We have a deep and abiding pride in the reputation of our great state.
As a country, the United States has a reputation for fairness, friendship, and freedom.
The Statue of Liberty is our symbol, beckoning the "tired and hungry" from far away lands to share our abundant life.
Each state is a little nation unto itself. The geography may change, the accent may differ, but a possessive pride for a nation of free men draws all 50 states into a binding respect for a united statehood.

Michigan is our current favorite.
She's been on our favorite state list as number one for a good many years. We're pleased and eager to share a little bit of her with every out-of-state person who crosses her boundaries.
She's a grand state!
We suggest you get better acquainted! There's still time to chart a late summer or early fall tour of our state. It will be a happy ending to a glorious summer time fairy-tale of fun and beauty.

Recipe Of The Week
Chocolate Chip Kisses
1/2 cup sweetened condensed milk
1 1/2 cups shredded coconut
1 /2 tsp baking powder
1 cup chocolate pieces
Combine condensed milk, coconut, and baking powder. Add chocolate pieces and drop from teaspoons onto greased baking sheet. Bake in slow oven, 325 deg for 25 minutes or until browned around edges. Makes 2 dozen.

MUSINGS OF A HOMEMAKER
By Mary Anne Tuck
August 16, 1962
(Houghton Lake Resorter)
Houghton Lake, Michigan

Factual Propaganda!

The Soviet Union has once more succeeded in providing a reluctant and
complacent "free world" with a masterpiece of "factual propaganda."

While some of our most respected and progressive minded state senators
conducted endless filibusters in deadlocked debate over an outer space,
government controlled "space communications" network, Russia
continue to bombard us with undeniable magnificent advances in the
current "space-race."
Most of us are content to ignore, as much as possible,
the daily reports of peace talks with the Reds. It appears we are sadly
lacking in the mastery of space in comparison to the USSR, so we panic.

We are disbelieving, angered and bewildered; faced with the grim fact an
industrially retarded nation such as Soviet Russia can beat our free and
democratic society in such an important area as the exploration of space.
We've listened to, read about, and watched with mounting despair the
multi-orbital flight of the two, now world renowned, "cosmonauts."

We've all but forgotten the achievement in question in favor of the race
to be first.
It seems to have become an obvious, if often overlooked, habit of the
American people to become so involved in the game
they lose sight of the ultimate objective.
It's discouraging to feel after decades of war and unrest between nations,
there is now the imminent danger of a contest for the control of space.
We're on the verge of a discovery, about which no one is certain.
Possibilities are beyond present comprehension even to the most learned

scientists.
To consider the situation in its entirety would be difficult for the imagination of the average person. Yet, once again, the need is evident for community understanding at the level of town and country.

To understand the complexities of space is almost impossible, but to understand neighbors and friends and earthly failings of human nature, is a primary necessity.
We would all profit from a little well placed community togetherness and more effort toward a great people to people network of communication.

Recipe Of The Week
This week's recipe was given to us by Mrs. Ron Smith of Houghton Lake.
It's called Cry Babies (Cookies)
1 1/2 cups brown sugar
2/3 cup shortening
1 egg
1 to 1 1/2 cups molasses
1/2 tsp ginger
1/2 cup cold coffee
1 tsp soda
4 1/2 cups flour
1 tsp cinnamon
1/2 tsp cloves
Mix ingredients together..Bake at 350 deg 1-12 minutes

MUSINGS OF A HOMEMAKER
By Mary Anne Tuck
December 1962
(Houghton Lake Resorter)
Houghton Lake, Michigan

The time is near...
The long awaited holiday is but a few days away.
The promise of a visit from St. Nicholas is about to be fulfilled, and the
kids are blissfully anticipating Christmas morning.

Gifts have been thoughtfully purchased, cards have been mailed, and
homes have been colorfully decorated.

Christmas dinner has been duly planned, Mom and Dad have set aside a
night for gift wrapping, and neighbors and friends are exchanging holiday
visits. A cup of steaming coffee, a slice of tantalizing fruit cake and good
conversation complete the bill of fare for delightful
pre-Christmas evenings.
The deeper, religious meaning of this approaching holiday is apparent to
all; with an inner glimpse of hope, faith, and the wonderful love since the
beginning of time.

The infinite love of our Lord was expressed so beautifully by the greatest
gift of all time; a tiny baby to lead the way to eternal peace.

On this Christmas day in the year of our Lord 1962, as the gifts are
exchanged and family gathers around for a day of warmth and love, may
we all remember the significance of this most joyous of all holidays.

In His Name, may the inner contentment you seek, the joy you feel, the
love you give, be with you and remain with you throughout the New
Year.

1963
Musings

MUSINGS OF A HOMEMAKER
By Mary Anne Tuck
January 1963
(Houghton Lake Resorter)
Houghton Lake, Michigan

The state of the union is good!
The future of our citizens is hopeful.
The best news of all is that we may soon experience a tax decrease.

In his State of the Union message, our President made the past sound distant, the present passing fair, and the future more promising than usual.
According to J.F.K., to retain our position of leadership in an ever changing world, we must continue to develop and maintain the inner security and outward appearance which only a free and successful nation may pose.
Every city, town and four-corner metropolis has a duty to the face of a nation; let it never be said the greatest little town of its kind fell short on its civic duty and national pride.
Tip-Up-Town U.S.A. provided a healthy, (if somewhat out of focus), eye opener to the waiting world.
It's over! It's done! Tip-Up-Town was ready for the world, but was the world ready for Tip-Up-Town?
If ever free elections, free enterprise, (free loading), and freedom of fun reigned supreme, it was never equaled by the whacky week-end when Tip-Up-Town put in its annual appearance.
Last week-end was a pleasurable time for visitors and residents alike.
The state of the nation was good, the state of the weather was cold, all systems were go and the outlook was A-Ok.
According to all indications we've recently celebrated the best Tip-Up-Town week-end on record!
Recipe For The Week
Kix Kandy
2 2/3 cup Kix

1/2 cup salted peanuts (or walnuts)
1/12 cup coconut
1/2 cup sugar
1/2 cup cream or top milk
11/4 cup corn syrup

Mix Kix, nuts and coconut (if desired) in bowl. Combine sugar cream and syrup in saucepan and cook to 236 deg stirring occasionally to prevent scorching. Remove from heat. Pour over Kix mixture and mix well. Flatten into butter 8"pan. Cool

MUSINGS OF A HOMEMAKER
By Mary Anne Tuck
January 10, 1963
(Houghton Lake Resorter)
Houghton Lake, Michigan

It's out of reach...

never to return again; ahead lies another, clean, new, and untouched.

It's the old year, of course; and the New Year is just ahead.

What's done is done; the simple truth is we've been given another chance. Hopefully it isn't a last chance, but an unmarked, unlisted, "re-run" over a course often traveled; but never the same way twice.

Success and failure, happiness and tears; with a backward glance, the months run together.

The year passed quickly, we say; but no more so than the year just ahead and each new year hereafter.

In the immediate future, right around home, we're pleasantly faced with plans for a happy week-end. There will be forty-eight hours crammed chock full of fun, visitors, and active relaxation.

The machinery which generates life into the framework of an ice bound "Tip-Up-Town USA", is even now being cleaned and oiled. (The better to run and carry out the intricate plans drawn up by the founding fathers of this now famous town.)

The mayor and marshal, after being elaborately sworn in, will take up residence on the town square to lend dignity and refinement to the festivities.

The population (no doubt the only one ever to be determined by a means other than government records), will depend entirely upon the ice, the weather and the ever abundant enthusiasm of all concerned.

Recent observations by civic-minded residents of the area may be somewhat bolstered by the obvious co-operation of the entire local population to make this annual affair a pleasant and prosperous success..

Recipe Of The Week

This week's recipe was given us by Mrs. Gordon Meinke of Meinke's Resort on the south shore of Houghton Lake.

She calls it, Cabbage Roll Ups and we call it "delicious". Hope you'll try it soon.

Cabbage Roll Ups

2 pounds hamburg

1 large onion

1 cup rice

2 eggs

1/2 cup catsup

Cabbage leaves

1 qt tomato juice

Cook hamburger in large fry pan along with chopped onion. Cook rice, and add to hamburger along with eggs. Stir in catsup. Soak cabbage leaves for 5 minutes in boiling water. After they have cooled enough to handle, spoon hamburger mixture into them. Then roll cabbage leaves around mixture and secure with two or more toothpicks. Place in bottom of roasting pan and pour 1 quart tomato juice over the top. Cover and bake 1 1/2 hours at 325 deg.

MUSINGS OF A HOMEMAKER
By Mary Anne Tuck
February 1963
(Houghton Lake Resorter)
Houghton Lake, Michigan

February first is knocking at the door.
St. Valentine's Day is approaching and we've had Old Man Winter
around just long enough to tire of his bitter cold and relentless snow.
We breezed through the holidays with a smile and looked forward to our
mid-winter Tip-Up-Town week end with great anticipation.
But now, the fun is over; we're all ready for a mild case of spring fever.
Ground Hog Day is imminent and our thoughts and day dreams turn
helplessly toward sprouting tulips, green grass, and fresh warm spring
breezes.
The last few weeks of below zero temperatures have put a strain on our
heating systems, our nerves, and our good humor.
Even the most unpleasant situation has a bright side for some. The fuel
man could hardly complain about "business opportunities" during the
recent cold wave. The men in the wrecker business have had "capacity
days", (and nights), and the winter sports parks are attracting hardy
adventure seeking crowds that delight in "down hill slalom" and "fast"
fills with just the right powder base.
Ice fishermen are finding a comfortable heated shanty a veritable must,
the fish are biting; that's as good a reason as any for braving the freezing
air day after day.
We may dream of sunny Florida where temperatures are normally high,
but even that southern state had had its share of dropping mercury.
Weather reports of the past few days have shown 85 degrees to be the
norm in Southern Florida; we must admit it's tempting.
Just last week, Houghton Lake admitted another resident to its ice-bound
shores. Their previous home was Florida. Their reason for moving, they
like the winters in northern Michigan. They are relatives of our editor
and wife and they've left sunny Florida in preference to a new home in
Michigan.

With such desire for this chilly climate from an out-of-stater, we may feel somewhat satisfied with this frozen, snow-bound Water Wonderland we choose to call home.

Welcome to Mr. And Mrs. Ed Wedding and family to Houghton Lake's wonders and weather.

Recipe For The Week
Baked Corn Pudding
2 cups corn
1 cup milk
1 tsp salt
2 eggs beaten
1/8 tsp pepper

Put corn in a greased baking dish. Combine eggs, milk, and seasonings. Put this mixture over corn and bake in a pan set in boiling water at 400 degrees for 40 minutes. Note: Cream style corn may be used. Yield; 6 servings

MUSINGS OF A HOMEMAKER
By Mary Anne Tuck
April 1963
(Houghton Lake Resorter)
Houghton Lake, Michigan

If the robin seems a little forlorn...
And the tender young buds on the trees and shrubs seem to labor under
a blanket of white, there's no need to check your calendar.
It's April all right! Late April at that.
Nature is very much in control of her playground.
Your tulips may be six inches high, your windows may have screens on
them, but that cold white stuff is present once more. We've greeted it
with somewhat less than overwhelming joy.
We are sure it won't be around for long; it's "white shoe" season already;
but for as long as it lasts, it's on with the boots, the mittens, the hats , car
heaters and window scrapers.
Since the early departure of the ice from winter chilled waters, awakening
tremors of springtime vigor have been evident to the practiced eye.
Resort owners are giving a refresher course to cottage and motels; boats
are getting a face lift with a new coat of paint. They'll afford happy
transportation for the patient fishermen from near and far.
Conventions are in the making. Banquets are shaping up and summer
vacation plans are sifting into the family conversation.
We've waited through a deadly, cold winter with ever present
expectations of a delightful spring and a pleasant summer.
One more month of school and the youngsters will be home for a busy
summer of playing, planning and growing.
We may have been revisited by "old man winter" on his way north for
the summer; springtime visits are short and summer is next in line.
May flowers, summer drives, shade trees and picnics;
Spring Fever survives and thrives.
Recipe Of The Week
Beef and Corn Shepherds Pie
2 tblsp cooking oil

1 lb ground beef
1 can cream style corn
1 1/2 tsp salt
1 tsp Worcestershire Sauce
1 tsp seasoned salt
2 tblsp minced parsley
1/8 tsp pepper
2 tsp minced onion
1 box instant mashed potatoes
4 eggs
1/2 cup milk

Heat cooking oil in skillet and saute beef until browned. Add corn, 1 tsp salt, Worcestershire Sauce, parsley, pepper, onion and mix lightly. Spread in greased 2 quart oblong baking dish. Spread potatoes over mix. Beat eggs, milk, salt, and pour over potatoes. Sprinkle with seasoned salt. Bake 400 deg. For 30 minutes or until golden brown.

MUSINGS OF A HOMEMAKER
By Mary Anne Tuck
May 1963
(Houghton Lake Resorter)
Houghton Lake, Michigan

Welcome to May!

Apple blossom time, spring lambs and speckled fawns; with optimistic foresight we hope we've seen the last of the snow for several months to come.

This is a perfect time for the greatest state in the union to proclaim her bountiful attractions to the remaining 49.

Michigan Week is but one of the May milestones. May Day, Mother's Day, graduation; this is a perfect month for appreciation.

The coming of summer, a day for showing Mother how much we love her, pride in our native state; it's a busy month fondly known as the "Merry Month of May".

That rich and inviting carpet of green on lawns and fields presents a thought or two of quite another nature.

The family lawn mower may need an overhaul. The left over leaf department may need an extra hour or two of "applied therapy", and the garden tiller will get an early workout in the garden spots; an advance scout for flowers and vegetables to grace our living in the months ahead. If your ambition is dragging its heels and your spouse is urging you on to bigger and better endeavors, just double check your May calendar and give it a mighty whirl.

Bowling season is over, golf is just beginning, the swim suit season is approaching zero hour; we're ready to go.

Our promise of "Summer Theater" entertainment has given area residents added incentive. The progress of this northern community during the past decade, has proven to be an interesting lesson in applied community effort.

We're glad we live in Michigan; how about you?

MUSINGS OF A HOMEMAKER
By Mary Anne Tuck
May 1963
(Houghton Lake Resorter)
Houghton Lake, Michigan

It's your day again Mom!

One day a year hardly seems enough to proclaim the love and affection
we hold for the gal to whose apron strings we'd "most like to be tied".

We can never repay, nor does Mom expect us to, the hours of love,
labor and devotion so happily bestowed on little heads.

How many times have childhood cares of monumental stature been
patiently reduced to molehills a child could easily climb beside a
thoughtful, caring Mother?

"Mother is here"; with that comforting knowledge we've had the courage
to face the seemingly insurmountable challenges of growing up, giving
and finding new love and new challenges.

From diapers to dates it's Mom to whom we turned for competent care
and cautious advice. Marriage and family may change our impressions of
Mom from what is expected of her to "how did she ever manage?"
Our ever changing times have altered the role of motherhood, to a
degree; the working Mother has gained an opportunity to express her
personal need for fulfillment outside the home.
We like to think, though, these working outside the home Mothers have
found a satisfactory way of rounding out the home in the ways only a
Mother can.
When all is said and done, whether she works outside or stays at home,
whether she's young and vigorous or silver-haired and contented, she's
"Mom". We're mighty glad when He sent our "Mom" He cared enough
to send the very best.

Recipe of the Week

Take one wonderful Mom, add one wonderful day, mix well, and treat her to a delicious dinner of her choice in the restaurant of her choice, and wish her a most happy "Mother's Day".
(This recipe will turn out equally as good if prepared by a devoted husband to the Mother of his children.)

MUSINGS OF A HOMEMAKER
By Mary Anne Tuck
July 1963
(Houghton Lake Resorter)
Houghton Lake, Michigan

How could we possibly be bored with this fair land of ours in the midst
of a beautiful July?

We've been treated too prolonged periods of high 80 degree weather,
dry spells, wet spells, hail stones, thunderstorms, driving rain and high
winds.
Pick and choose, if you will.
With such an assortment from which to choose, one scarcely feels the
need for making special weather requests. The curiosity of each day's
weather is a pleasure to anticipate. (?)
We've been privileged to enjoy a duke's mixture of summer fun. For the
first time in many years there's more to June, July and August than hot
weather, hard work, and kids.
We've always looked forward to outdoor eating, cool evenings and fresh,
clean air. We finally made a visit to Hazen's Isle, and the river boat in
process. We had a bird's eye view of the fireworks on the 4th and the
Playhouse; for the second year, simply grand!
We've yet to go for a ride without seeing deer; been treated to close ups
of lumbering turkeys, bandit raccoons and the lightning quick, red fox.
A three and one half hour drive, following yellow markers, took us past
many sights; the Experimental Stations deer pens; tiny, quiet fawns and
magnificent bucks in velvet.
We've tried looking at Houghton Lake as objectively as a vacationer
might.
We saw pleasant skies, rippling blue water, and mile upon mile of green
forests.
We saw stands of virgin timber as we listened intently to the stillness,
utter stillness of the mid-forest trails.
At first glance, upon arrival in the community, we see resorts and motels,

restaurants, more resorts, more motels, and signs, and signs, and more signs.

We begin to meet the friendly natives and pleasant folks who call Houghton Lake, home.

We slowly become immune to the sight of continuously beckoning advertisements on main highways and feel only the comfort and solitude in the surrounding miles of unmarked forests.

There's a change of pace, a relaxing difference, a fitting and proper place for vacationing; Houghton Lake, Roscommon County, Michigan.

Recipe Of The Week

Chewy Peanut Butter Bars

1/3 cup shortening

1/4 cup firmly packed light brown sugar

1 cup granulated sugar

1 tsp vanilla

1 cup unsifted flour

1tsp baking powder

1 1/3 cup coconut

1/2 cup peanut butter

2 eggs

1/4 tsp salt

Cream together shortening, peanut butter, and sugars until light and fluffy. Add vanilla and eggs, beat well. Mix in flour, baking powder, and salt, stirring only until blended. Stir in coconut. Spread evenly in greased 13x9x2 inch pan. Bake in 350 deg oven about 25 minutes or until golden brown. Cut into bars. Makes 36

MUSINGS OF A HOMEMAKER
By Mary Anne Tuck
July 1963

And the rains came...
The crops grew, the vacationers arrived and everyone lived happily ever after, almost.
The kids are suffering from mid-summer doldrums, the Moms are suffering from midsummer kids, and the Dads; well, they're just suffering.
Miss Universe of 1962 has relinquished her crown to the beautiful successor. Miss America is preparing to become a lovely "has been", and the average housewife is midway between freezing strawberries and canning peaches; wondering when she'll ever find the time to acquire that dreamed of summer tan all her friends are sporting.
Summer seems to have changed since those bygone days when "Hector was a pup", or maybe we're the ones who have changed.

Summertime used to mean watermelons and homemade ice cream, the old swimming hole, Sunday picnics, endless days of sunshine and fun, and evenings of twinkling stars and relaxation.
Nowadays, we've noticed a definite trend toward peanut butter sandwiches and popsicles, plastic wading pools and front yard lunches, endless days of small fry and dirty clothes, evenings of "reruns", and frankly "done in", worn out, and ready to retire...home folks.
At a closer inspection, it's evident most definite changes have come about.
With the oncoming years, it becomes more evident the give and take fluctuates with age. The younger years are the taking years, with everything from sunshine to 'ours for the asking". Then the giving years, the real, honest to goodness "living years", when we learn the real pleasures in doing and planning and giving to those for whom we care the most.
Recipe of the Week
Gumdrop Cookies

4 eggs
1 tblsp cold water
1/4 tsp salt
1/2 cup chopped nuts
2 cups brown sugar
2 cups flour
1 tsp cinnamon
1 cup shredded gumdrops

Beat eggs and sugar and water and mix well. Sift flour, salt and cinnamon; add nuts and gumdrops. Add this to sugar mix. Spread thin in greased and floured shallow pan. Bake in 325 deg oven for 30 minutes. Ice while warm.

Icing
3 tblsp butter
2 tblsp orange juice
1 tsp grated orange rind
Powdered sugar.

Cut in squares and remove from pan when cool.

MUSINGS OF A HOMEMAKER
By Mary Anne Tuck
August 1963
(Houghton Lake Resorter)
Houghton Lake, Michigan

The last month of summer is upon us..
Like it or not, this grand and glorious season is drawing to a close.
We have come to look upon the eighth month as the hottest month of
summer, heaven help our dampened brows if this year proves to be no
exception.
Pardon us for being trite and talking about the weather, but we've really
been a bit over conscious of the mercurial depth of late.
The carpet is pathworn between the television and the radio. The only
time we really listen intently is during the weather forecast.
Mr. Big on our nicest people list is the dear gentleman at the
Roscommon County Weather Station who said, and we quote, "not so
humid on Tuesday". Can you blame us for our hero worship? This
man, figuratively speaking, saved us from the humidity and promised to
make Monday evening more bearable; he promised us better days ahead.
We've heard of a little town called Parker in the state of Arizona. It is
reputed to be the "hottest little town in the nation". The 1,650 people
who reside in Parker remember a day in 1935 when the mercury hit 127
degrees.
Are we complaining? Well...we who live in the grand old state of
Michigan are used to living on the top of the heap; a minimum of bugs, a
maximum of wildlife, a wide claim on the "not too much" area on the
thermometer.
It's warmer and cooler, elsewhere. To top it off, we have a liberal dash of
industry, counter balanced with woods and waters.
We muse, at times, as to whether the people who've moved from
Northern Michigan to other states, are satisfied with what we like to think
of as "second best".
Have you guessed? We're stuck on our state; summer, fall, winter,
spring; we like what Michigan has to offer.

Recipe Of The Week

We ran across this salad idea in a current magazine. We tried it and it was delicious. How about giving it a whirl..it goes great with cold cuts or hot dogs or hamburgs. Just what you need to spruce up a wilted appetite.

Molded Fruit Salad

2 envelopes unflavored gelatin

1 cup cold water

1 can 6oz frozen lemonade concentrate

1 can fruit cocktail

1 cup salad dressing

Sprinkle gelatin on water in saucepan. Stir constantly over low heat, about 3 minutes, till gelatin dissolves. Remove from heat. Add unthawed concentrate; stir till melted. Gradually blend fruit cocktail syrup into creamy salad dressing; blend in lemonade mix. Chill till mixture mounds when dropped from spoon. Fold in fruit; turn into 6 cup mold. Chill firm. Unmold

MUSINGS OF A HOMEMAKER
By Mary Anne Tuck
September 1963
(Houghton Lake Resorter)
Houghton Lake, Michigan

The call of the great outdoors...
may not be your cup of tea. Your spouse may not cotton to the idea of
society dances and bridge dates; so if you have the urge to get a little
additional exercise and want to make it a family affair, why not take the
kids for an evening of fun and try bowling?
As a family sport, bowling is sweeping the nation. The grade school set
can enjoy the game as well as Grandma and Grandpa.
As is so often the case, when husband and wife are searching for a mutual
interest in recreation, an evening out at the bowling alley may prove to be
an eye-opener for friendly competition with a common objective.
It's great to see the teenagers take an interest in the game too.
In an area such as ours, where the fun possibilities for the teenage set are
limited, it's encouraging to note that bowling is right up their alley.
It's an inexpensive, clean game of skill and luck; intriguing to all who
attempt to master the art.
We've worried, more than a little, about the seemingly fading family
togetherness of years gone by.
We've been deluged with articles in magazines and programs on
television and radio about the lack of parental participation in teenage
guidance. We might make an amendment to the "guidance" angle of the
teenage dilemma. Try a little "leading" in its place.
Instead of "telling" our kids where to find their fun, why not show them?
Take the whole family bowling and see for yourself!
Recipe For The Week
No Bake..Peanut Butter and Oatmeal Cookies
2 cups sugar
1 tsp vanilla
1/4 cup cocoa
1/2 cup milk

1 stick margarine or butter

Mix above ingredients together and cook hard, 1 1/2 minutes, then add 3 cups quick cooking oats and 3/4 cup peanut butter. Stir thoroughly and drop by teaspoon on wax paper and allow to set until cold.

MUSINGS OF A HOMEMAKER

By Mary Anne Tuck
September 1963
(Houghton Lake Resorter)
Houghton Lake, Michigan

With the onset of a new school term,
We homemakers are noting a distinct and fairly new addition to morning
television viewing.
If pre-schoolers still provide the patter of not so tiny feet in your home,
then perhaps you've been startled to hear the sound of the classroom
immediately following early morning children's programs.
Television classrooms are certainly not new to most of us, but we think
they merit a closer look.
American history never looked or sounded as good in high school (to
this writer) as it does on these TV Classrooms for today's young scholars.
The dry, but factual pages in textbooks of the past, cannot compare with
this vivid picture as painted by the notably silver-toned television teachers
chosen for space age teaching methods.
It's a well known, though discouraging fact, many of us get more than a
little stale as an ever widening span separates us from well spent years of
schooling.
Just as a doctor keeps his hands agile, and a teacher takes refresher
courses, shouldn't we "home-managing" experts remain alert to the
current trends in texts and sciences as taught under the guise of the "3
Rs" and the "Golden Rule"?
Although we've no compiled data on hand to view the results of this new
approach to teaching, we believe it is a meaningful and promising new
aspect to the centuries old privilege of instilling the basic abilities in
youngsters; necessary for a fulfilling and rewarding adult life.
If you haven't tuned in on one of these morning classrooms, we'd like to
suggest you give it a whirl!

MUSINGS OF A HOMEMAKER

By Mary Anne Tuck
September 1963
(Houghton Lake Resorter)
Houghton Lake, Michigan

Mmm..The tantalizing flavor of fall is in the air.
It's a brisk, invigorating aroma; a promise of burning leaves, a touch of
Jack Frost, and cheering throngs of spectators in the clutches of exciting
football games.
Small game seasons are approaching and hunters are experiencing
familiar yearnings for snappy October mornings, dew laden fields, and
promising hedge-rows holding pheasants for man and dog.
The wily game birds of Northern and Southern Michigan provide a
worthy quest for both hunter and "friend".
Color tours, having become a major Michigan fall pastime, will soon
reach a brilliant climax of russet and gold, orange and scarlet; undeniable
beauty in the eye of any beholder.
An exhilarating change of pace is unfolding. Ahead, are many weeks (we
hope) of lazy Indian Summer days when we can set aside the persistent
knowledge that "Old Man Winter" is readying himself for a visit. Jack
Frost really means business, despite his transforming touch, painting field
and forest with brilliant hues of fall finery.
The annual, and most definite sign, of approaching hunting seasons is the
mysterious appearance of objects scattered across the lake; the results of
hours of hard work by enterprising resort operators. The impressive bulk
of this necessary evil to the duck hunting sportsman, is but one of the
more positive forecast of days ahead; the duck blinds are out, providing
anxious hunters convenient cover.
If the man of the house at your address is an avid sportsman, it might be
a good idea to see if you can talk him into putting away the lawn
furniture, putting up the storm windows, now. If hunting is a must for
him, prepare yourself. It's time for a change of seasons.
It's autumn in this great state of Michigan.
Recipe For The Week

We can thank Mrs. Alice Hamp this week for sharing with us a recipe for
Pralines From New Orleans
1 cup white sugar
1 cup brown sugar
2 cups pecans
1/3 stick butter
1/3 cup boiling water
Pinch of salt
1 tsp vanilla

Boil 6 minutes, *watch the clock*. Beat 1 minute, *watch the clock*. Drop by spoonfuls on waxed paper. Paper should be on cutting board, they cool better and are easier to pick off waxed paper.

We want to hear from you readers and share your favorite recipes.
Just send them care of The Resorter.

MUSINGS OF A HOMEMAKER
By Mary Anne Tuck
October 1963
(Houghton Lake Resorter)
Houghton Lake, Michigan

What are we doing to our schools?

Have we personally boycotted our local schools with unintentional neglect? Have we willfully crippled the education of our children through gross unconcern and minimum effort?
Our community, through the years, has suffered growing pains of average intensity for an area with the size and wealth of Houghton Lake. We've moaned and groaned, then pulled ourselves up by our bootstraps to a level of enviable quality for any school system in any area of equal proportions.
We have maintained enough taxes which which to provide our schools a satisfactory amount of funds; now, as our community has grown, so has our school population. It has increased to the bursting point.
Through mass distribution of the media, or worse yet, no information at all; we have succeeded in dropping our potential educational resources to practically nothing with a promise of "worse to come".
We have wisely availed ourselves of a truly competent administration, a frankly interested Board Of Education, and a highly trained teaching staff; only to "nip in the bud"any hope of progress in providing sufficient and adequate classroom facilities for our growing needs.
In so doing, we have tentatively severed any hope of maintaining operational funds upon which we will be asked to vote before another school year is over.
When we consider the past, refusal after refusal to vote taxes needed for our schools, it would seem to indicate, (consciously or unconsciously), depending on the individual, a desire for stunted growth in the area of education.
We may look forward to half-day sessions, three days per week classes and one teacher for every 35 or 40 children.

If you've had youngsters of your own, or have been close to the children of others, then we're confident you realize what an appalling idea those classroom conditions brings to mind.
What can we do about this unacceptable situation?
Give it some honest thought, that's all you can ask of yourself.
THEN, ACT UPON YOUR CONVICTIONS!

Recipe For The Week
Apple Pineapple Pie
2 cups sifted flour
1 tsp salt
1 egg yolk
2 tsp lemon juice
2/3 cup shortening
Blend flours, salt, and shortening as usual Blend egg, lemon juice and about 4 tblsp water and sprinkle over flour. Mix and roll out.
Filling
4 cups apples sliced or 1 can apples
1 cup crushed pineapple undrained
2/3 cup sugar 3 tblsp flour
1 tsp cinnamon
1 tblsp melted butter
Combine ingredients, gently pour into lined pastry pan. Brush top crust with butter. Bake 10 minutes at 425 deg..then 350 deg. For 25-30 minutes

MUSINGS OF A HOMEMAKER
By Mary Anne Tuck
October 1963
(Houghton Lake Resorter)
Houghton Lake, Michigan

The leaves are fluttering to the ground.

Much of the brilliant autumn coloring is lying in thick layers of woodland carpet

Fall is slipping through our fingers just as surely as the warm summer days. We can't encourage it to linger; there are many colorful and busy days just ahead with which to entice the hunter, the skier and the patient fisherman.

Once more we are reminded of the ever changing scene in the nation's best loved, (we like to think), four-season vacation state.

During the past few weeks we've noticed increased activity by various associations throughout our area. The year around residents have begun to channel their labors in a Civic minded direction after a long summer of "shoulder to the wheel", 18-hour days.

The community has taken a keen interest in the renewed effort to build a new high-school football team after a season of inactivity. The school spirit is evident among young folks and adults alike.

The Parent-Teacher Associations, nation-wide, are back in the swing of things once more; providing a pleasant atmosphere in which to promote a better understanding between parent and teacher.

Many of us become, for one reason or another, somewhat reticent to be involved in community projects; PTA and various other clubs and organizations.

We might take an astronaut's eye view of the situation and note that from afar, this world in which we live is really not so large and imposing as one might think.

Even the most minute contribution of time, knowledge, and a helping hand is needed, important, and appreciated.

During this radically changing season, when nature herself is storing against the onslaught of winter, we might try adding at least one "acorn" of much needed rations against the possibility of failure by well meaning groups who need your help.

The harvest of a crop planted with a drop of compassion is sure to bring much personal satisfaction.

Recipe Of The Week

Our recipe for this week is a timely one, sent to us by Mrs. Ralph Blouch, of Houghton Lake.

Pheasant In Sour Cream

Cut up two pheasants which have been properly aged by "hanging" in the plumage for several days. Dredge pieces in flour and saute in butter or olive oil. Use a Dutch oven or heavy skillet with lid. Add 1/2 cup chopped green onions and 1 can or 1/2 lb mushrooms. Pour over the mixture 2 ounces of bourbon or white wine and season with salt and pepper. Add enough broth made from chicken bouillon cube from time to time so pheasant doesn't burn. Simmer gently, covered, for about one hour or till tender. Add a tsp of MSG (Accent) and about 10 minutes before serving, stir in 1/2 point sour cream. Heat through and serve.

Many thanks to Helen for "something different" in pheasants.

MUSINGS OF A HOMEMAKER
By Mary Anne Tuck
November 1963
(Houghton Lake Resorter)
Houghton Lake, Michigan

Parent-Teacher conferences are approaching...
a dynamic departure from days gone by when the shortest (and often
only) pipeline between John or Mary's teacher and Mom and Dad was
the somewhat biased opinion of the student in question; based mostly, we
think, on a theory of self preservation.
Many are the youngsters of yesteryear who planted a deep-rooted
mistrust between parent and teacher by simply not telling the entire
circumstance surrounding a classroom situation.
Unfortunately, in that case, it is a completely human reaction to take the
word of our loved one in place of one whom we've never met; though the
knowledge of our years should tell us of the wandering mind of the
normal child who finds himself in a wee bit of hot water...so to speak.
Parent-Teacher conferences have afforded an excellent and reliable
approach toward a better understanding between Johnny's Mom and
Dad and Johnny's teacher; with this approach the margin for error
between what happens at school and what is told at home, may diminish
almost entirely.
We are consulted as to our preference of the hour for the meeting, given
the full time and attention of our child's teacher, and an opportunity to
learn exactly how our own child is progressing.
Many communities, equipped for such classes, are now teaching courses
in bowling and skiing along with the usual sports of baseball, basketball,
football and track.
To the casual (and not too interested) observer, the need for extra-
curricular activities is not apparent. We wonder how many industrious
"book-worm" students have found it extremely difficult to make social
adjustments after high school years spent solely in the company of non-
competitive textbooks companions.
We noticed recently in grade-school, a tasting party was held for first and

second graders to sample different types of foods. Any Mom who claims relationship to an elementary school child, should certainly commend this method of encouraging them to try something new in foods.
All in all, it looks like a new era in teaching methods and teacher-parent activities is well on its way. We're for it one hundred percent.
We think you'll be pleased and gratified if you enter into these new ides with open minds and all out encouragement for the fine efforts of the teachers and administrators of our community schools.

Recipe For The Week
Oatmeal Date Nut Cake
1 cup boiling water
1/2 cup dates
1 cup quick cooking rolled oats
2 eggs, beaten
1 cup sifted flour
1 cup brown sugar
1 tsp soda
1/2 cup white sugar
1 tsp salt
1/2 cup shortening
1 tsp cinnamon
1/2 cup nuts
1/2 tsp cloves

Pour boiling water over rolled oats..Mix sugar, shortening and eggs, add dates and nuts. Combine flour, soda, cinnamon, cloves and salt. Mix oat mixture and egg mixture; beat. Add flour Bake in 350 deg oven for 35 minutes

MUSINGS OF A HOMEMAKER
By Mary Anne Tuck
November 1963
(Houghton Lake Resorter)
Houghton Lake, Michigan

Opening day...from year to year.
The deer hunting sportsman waits, with pleasant anticipation, the "crack
of dawn" on November fifteenth; opening day of the Michigan deer
hunting season.
Northern Michigan attracts, each year, thousands of red clad sportsmen
in quest of the mighty White-tail Deer.
Through colorful and reminiscent tales told by the "Old Timers", we
know of years gone by when the deer herd was magnificent and the
antlered buck was always a sight to behold.
The Michigan Conservation Department has endeavored to solve the
problem of the dwindling White-tail population through methods quite
widely questioned by many sportsman's clubs and individual hunters.
Although the plight of the herd is foremost in the minds of all concerned,
bitter and somewhat heated verbal battles have resulted in widening the
gap between the professional Conservation person and the rightly
concerned (if unstudied) hunter.
Amidst the heat of debate, comes the season itself, when some will return
home victorious and happy (and not so sure the Conservation
Department was wrong), while others will return empty-handed, defeated,
and all the more positive the Department is traveling a road to positive
failure. They will return home to fight the battle with renewed vigor.
Never-the-less, the true deer hunter will set out on this opening day with
great anticipation for the hunt, regardless of the outcome.
The quiet trail, the cracking twig, the thrilling glimpse of a bounding
White-tail will always spell "deer season" to the hunter; the memory of
which, brings him North year after year.
Recipe Of The Week
We were most pleased to hear from Mrs. K.W. Kime, Sr., of Toledo,
Ohio, who sent us a most interesting recipe for Fruit Cake Cookies; with

a well timed suggestion we might take a moment to remember someone's loved one in any State Hospital, or a Veteran, with something we've baked for the Holiday Season.

Fruit Cake Cookies

Bake at 375 degrees 20 minutes   Yield 8 dozen

1/2 cup butter

1 cup dark brown sugar

1/4 cup jelly (currant or apple)

2 eggs

2 tsp soda

2 tblsp orange juice of Cognac

2 cups sifted flour

1/2 tsp each of allspice, cloves, cinnamon, and nutmeg

1 pound pecans, chopped

1 pound seedless raisins

1 pound candied cherries, finely chopped

1 pound candied pineapple, finely chopped

1/2 pound citron, fine chopped

In a bowl, cream the butter until fluffy. Add the sugar and jelly. Beat until soft and fluffy. Add eggs, one at a time, beat well after each addition. Dissolve soda in juice. Add to creamed mix. Sift flour and spices; add half to the creamed mix. Dredge nuts and fruits with remaining flour mix. Stir into batter. Blend well. Drop by tbsp on to cookie sheets. Bake until firm on top. Remove to racks. Wrap cookies in aluminum foil. Store in cool place, or tightly covered can. let ripen as you would with a fruitcake. Occasionally sprinkle wine on top.

Many thanks to Mrs. Kime for the recipe! We hope you'll share your favorite holiday recipes with us.

MUSINGS OF A HOMEMAKER
By Mary Anne Tuck
November 1963
(Houghton Lake Resorter)
Houghton Lake, Michigan

With the holiday season virtually on our doorstep,
the time has come for some family conferences to determine the extent
to which our homes should be decorated.
Whether your family is one who begins and ends the holiday trimmings
with the Christmas tree; or one who decorates everything from the
mailbox to the kitchen sink, the entire operation is blessed with holiday
traditions.
One city, located to the south of us, has maintained a reputation through
the years as a town well worth visiting during the holiday season. Its
homes and business decorations are a sight to behold. Some are
intricately designed, while others have used only a string of lights and a
little imagination.
The over all result is worth the hour drive for the entire family.

Some years ago, the folks here at Houghton lake began to encourage
home owners to do some outside decorating.The result was much
original and industrious planning and a great deal of enjoyment for the
residents of the area.
The adage of old, "It is more blessed to give than to receive", is well
placed when applied to the practice of dressing up the outside of our
homes as well as the inside for friends and neighbors to receive your
unspoken greeting as they drive by or come to visit.

Local organizations have spent much time, money and energy to make
this unusual area of ours a better place for business and industry. A bit of
assistance from the individual could certainly add to the color and
atmosphere so diligently pursued by this community and others..
A red bow on the mail box, a wreath on the front door, Santa on the roof
or a string of lights in the window; the investment is small and the

dividends will be returned to the community, over and over. Why not load the family in the car some evening during this holiday season and go sight-seeing "right around home"; you'll be pleasantly surprised at the holiday hello from neighbor to neighbor.

Recipe For The Week

Steamed Cherry Pudding

1/2 cup shortening

1 cup sugar

2 eggs, beaten

2 1/2 cups sifted all-purpose flour

3 tsp. Baking powder

1/4 tsp salt

1 cup milk

2 cups canned sour cherries, drained

Cream the shortening and sugar and add the beaten eggs. Add the sifted dry ingredients alternately with the milk. Stir in the cherries. Fill Greased individual aluminum molds 2/3 full, cover with aluminum foil, and steam for one hour in a blancher. Place 2 quarts of water in bottom section of blancher. Serve with a cherry sauce. Serves 6-8

Cherry Sauce

1 cup cherry juice

1 1/2 tblsp cornstarch

1/4 cup sugar 1/4 cup cold water

1 tblsp butter

1/8 tsp almond extract

1 cup cherries

Bring cherry juice to boil in saucepan. Combine cornstarch, sugar and cold water and add to hot juice. Stir constantly until sauce boils. Remove from heat, cool slightly. Add butter, almond extract and cherries.

MUSINGS OF A HOMEMAKER
By Mary Anne Tuck
December 1963
(Houghton Lake Resorter)
Houghton Lake, Michigan

The seasonal pine tree stands in the corner..
Colorful but lonely.
Gaily wrapped gifts are no longer there.
Sweet scented boughs no longer hover over shiny new bicycles and curly haired dolls. The tree's annual mission has reached and passed its usefulness of breathtaking expectations. Glittering and once lovely wrappings lie crushed in empty cartons awaiting the inevitable trip to the incinerator; a most common destination for used gift wrappings no matter how treasured their contents may have been.

Mixed emotions may envelop our package of memories, sadness and laughter, hope and regret, faith and tenderness; a colorful display denoting 12 months of a very full life.

It's time to wrap up the old year; 1963 is ready to be decked with ribbons of memories; a length of red for the passion of living, blue for the richness of loving, gold for the bright rays of learning, and green for the promise of growing and new life in the coming year.
In retrospect the year has flown on humming bird's wings, never pausing for more than a fleeting moment, never taking more than a drop of the sweet nectar provided by the full blooming flower of life.
The new calendar is offering 12 long months ahead in which we will create a new package. Once more, at the end of the year, we'll store our accumulated memories.
We're starting anew. The final design will be original and personal, full of twists and turns and colorful hues which will shade the months ahead.
Gracious living to you and yours in the new year, 1964.
Recipe of the Week
From Mrs. Jerry Frantz Jr., Midland Michigan comes this recipe for

Frosted Jam Bars

Melt 1/2 cup butter or margarine; stir in 1/2 cup dark corn syrup. Mix in 1 beaten egg and 1/2 tsp. Vanilla

Sift together 1 1/2 cups sifted enriched flour, 1 tsp baking powder, 1/2 tsp salt and 1/2 tsp cinnamon; add to the syrup mix. Spread half the batter in greased 11 x 7 x 1 1/2 inch pan. Spoon 3/4 cup commercial strawberry preserves or jam over; carefully cover with remaining batter.

Bake in hot oven 400 deg 20-25 minutes. Frost while warm with confectioner sugar icing. Cool and cut in bars. Makes about 1 1/2 dozen.

MUSINGS OF A HOMEMAKER
By Mary Anne Tuck
1963
(Houghton Lake Resorter)
Houghton Lake, Michigan

Do we expect too much of our teen-agers?
Or do we take too much for granted?

Are we encouraging the "tween" set to meet difficulty with aggressive
curiosity or to conform to the inevitable, with passive forbearance?
In this space age in which we live, the fast moving society of conformity
and "isms" reeks more of expectability than sensibility.

Many a well adjusted and morally refined adult not only guides but
pushes his teenage charge toward a destination of inevitable disaster.
The delinquency of American youth is a problem of sizeable concern.

We realize it, we are aware of it, and yet the scene is set for teenage self-
destruction through unintentional but none the less disastrous, parental
irresponsibility.

From Junior High on, the teen-ager is allowed and expected to travel a
well trodden path from going steady to marriage at an increasingly young
age level.
From social science to infant care is hardly the well planned curriculum
for the 16 year old girl; equally sad is the inopportune advance from first
string football to second rate jobs available to the teen-age Dad with a
growing family to support.
Our community, under the guidance of our Junior High and High
School administrators, has recently been afforded a most important
opportunity to reinstate the Junior High group to a level of social activity
designed and directed toward the physical and emotional level for Junior
high boys and girls.
We're being given a second chance, at the local level, to correct the

improper approach which has been so commonly made in attitudes toward children.

It's worth more than a casual consideration. If we've lived long enough to have gained an insight of these mistakes, then we've lived long enough to know the personal touch to any situation is the most important one. Invest some time in the country's future, you've already invested your future in your children.

Recipe Of The Week

Graham Butterscotch Cookies

2 cups brown sugar

1 cup shortening (scant)

2 eggs

1 cup chopped raisins

1 cup graham flour

2 cups white flour

1/2 tsp salt

1 tsp vanilla

1 tsp soda

1 tsp baking powder

Cream shortening with sugar. Add eggs and raisins. Combine dry ingredients and add to mixture. Bake 8-12 minutes at 350 deg

1964
Musings

Musings of a Homemaker
By Mary Anne Tuck
May 1964

You can't stroll down our lane...
Without being overcome by the aroma of lilacs and apple blossoms.
Tiny, pale blossoms nod gently in the spring breezes and lovely, pastel
pink buds are awaiting the moment of blossoming with single intent.

Sounds like something out of a book, doesn't it? Yet, it's an undeniably
apt description, if somewhat flowery, and it leads us to wonder if beauty
isn't in the 'ear" as well as the "eye" of the beholder.

We are inclined to be careless with phrases like "lovely", "cute", sweet"
and on down the gamut of adjectives. When we find something worth a
thought and a special word, the every day descriptions which we've
bandied around so carelessly seem cold, used and not very accurate.
We've become a nation of "adjective droppers".
Little girls are sweet. Cars are sweet. Dresses are sweet. Husbands are
sweet. Fishing rods are sweet.
Sugar is sweet.
The weather is lovely. Your wife is lovely. Your children are Lovely.
Dinner is lovely.
Boy friends are cute. Freckles are cute. Puppies are cute.
Babies are cute.
Everything from soup to nuts is sweet, cute and lovely. Where do we go
from here?
Teen-agers are juvenile delinquents. Juvenile delinquents are teen-agers.
Grandparents are gray-haired people.
Gray haired people are grandparents.
Explanatory phrases sometimes explain away so much we completely
lose sight of the picture.
But...if you walk down our drive-way and aren't absolutely thrilled by the
sweet smell of lilacs and apple blossoms in bloom; then it's neither your
"eye" nor your "ear" that's out of kilter my friend.

It's your nose.
If that turns out to be your problem, believe me when I tell you you're missing the very best part of spring!

Recipe of the Week
Hedgehogs
2 cups shelled walnuts
1 cup pitted dates
2 cups shredded moist coconut
1 cup brown sugar, firmly packed
2 eggs, slightly beaten
Put nuts and dates through food chopper, using coarse blade. Mix with 1 1/2 cup of the coconut, sugar and eggs. Shape into rolls about 3/4 inch thick and 2 inches long. Roll in the remaining 1/2 cup coconut. Place in greased baking sheet. Bake in 350 deg oven 10-12 minutes.

MUSINGS OF A HOMEMAKER
By Mary Anne Tuck
June 1964
(Houghton Lake Resorter)
Houghton Lake, Michigan

Is it really this wonderful, sunny, warm weather..
That makes us disagreeable, or are we just naturally hard to please?
Just a few short weeks ago we were pining for warm summer days. Now
that they've finally arrived, we wonder when it's going to "cool off".

It must be the nature of human beings to search for greener grass just
over the fence.
From the age of ten, we find ourselves wishing for things we don't have.
If only our name was John instead of George; if only my name was Susan
instead of Mary. How wonderful it must be to have beautiful red hair
instead of brown; blonde hair instead of brunette.
Oh for the privilege of being in third grade instead of second; on it goes
until we reach high school.
Now we yearn for a "steady date" and find, to our amazement, the
"steady daters" entertain visions of "playing the field" and dating around."
If the choice is not to attend college, we soon nurture envious thoughts of
those who "went on".
The bride who marries young may wish she had waited awhile and is
surprised to learn the mature bride often feels she wasted those precious
years before marriage.
The housewife wants a job outside the home and the working woman
longs for a "stay at home day" such as the ones her friends enjoy.

One would almost think we are a people overflowing with discontent
from childhood on, but such is not the case.
Although "keeping up with the Jones" has come to be an accepted way of
life by many, the butt of countless jokes by others is merely an expression
for uneasy feelings connected with the everlasting search for "greener
grass". It's a small part of the game, however; the game we've invented to

give ourselves a much needed incentive to strive for bigger and better things, material and spiritual.

When you hear your neighbor belaboring the fact the days are "much too long", the weather is "much to hot", " wonder what it's like in Alaska today"; just remember they are following the rules of the game.

The game is called, "Making Conversation".

The objective is to see how much better we can make everyday living even better by some good natured complaining and few constructive thoughts.

Let's see what each of us can do to make this land of ours an even more pleasant place in which to live!

Recipe of the Day

Pineapple Dessert

1 1/2 cups sugar

1/2 cup butter

3 eggs (separate yolk and white)

1 can crushed pineapple

3/4 cups graham crackers

Cream butter and sugar; add beaten egg yolks. Add drained pineapple. Fold in beaten egg white. Put half of crushed graham cracker crumbs in bottom of 9 x 13 inch size pan. Spread on the pineapple mixture, then put other half of crumbs over top. Chill for 5-6 hours and serve with whipped cream.

MUSINGS OF A HOMEMAKER
By Mary Anne Tuck
September 1964
(Houghton Lake Resorter)
Houghton Lake, Michigan

It's September
Obvious to each in a different way, depending on your niche in life.

The difference between summer and fall lies somewhere between
midnight August 31st and 12:01 September 1st; admittedly, this voyage
from summer to fall passes swiftly and is seldom witnessed by anyone
other than insomnia sufferers and sleep walkers.

The most reliable sign is on the calendar. August is followed by
September, eight is followed by nine; we're all agreed on this and this
alone. Henceforth, each travels his own avenue to the north winds.
One autumnal indication, which rarely fails, is the shallow depth of one's
bank account. This situation may be brought about in many different
ways; notorious methods include summer vacations, summer visitors,
summer wardrobes and summer food bills. Along with the meager
balance in the account by September 1st, one may reasonably include
future fall vacations, fall visitors, fall clothing and fall food bills.

Another unfailing method of determining summer's end is contained in
the difference in the weather between the two months.
This method, familiar to all, is easily identifiable since August is always
the hottest driest month and the thermometer never drops below 65
during her 31 nights of wide open windows and light weight blankets.
Record high temperatures are frequently set in August, but never record
lows, and you can count on that.
Kids are anxious to be back in school, especially those between the ages
of 12 and 16. Businessmen and women are relieved to see the end of the
"money making" season.
On almost any street corner, any gas station or soda fountain hang-out of

the local retailers, one may hear wistful comments about the days ahead when a relaxing work day may bring no more than three or four customers into any one business establishment.
Without these obviously accurate, outward signs of approaching fall, we could scarcely believe what the calendar knows to be true.
It is September. Obviously, the best still lies ahead.!

Recipe of the Day

No Yeast Coffee Cake

1 cup sugar   1/4 cup butter   2 eggs   2 cups sifted flour 1 tsp soda
1 tsp baking powder   1 cup sour cream ground nuts

Topping

1 tsp cinnamon   1/2 cup sugar

Cream sugar and butter, add eggs, flour, soda and baking powder. Add sour cream and blend well. Put half of batter in angel food cake pan. Sprinkle 1/2 of topping over mixture. Pour remaining batter over topping and sprinkle with rest of sugar mixture. sprinkle with nuts and bake at 350 deg for 40 minutes

My New Year Resolutions
1964
"I Know Better"

"The time has come', the walrus said, "to speak of many things, of sailing ships and sealing wax and cabbages and kings" (and my New Year resolutions.)

Each of us, in the back of our mind, is guilty of harboring "*I know better*" feelings which emerge every year on January 1st.

(These feelings become submerged on January 2 or thereabout.)

* * * * * * * * * * * *

For instance. "*I know better*" than to let the ironing pile up week after week. while stashing the clothes I like to do least in a separate basket. When that basket overwhelms my utility room, the guilt sets in.

Therefore: I resolve to keep my ironing up to date.

"*I know better*" than to chide my friends in far off places for not being regular in their correspondence with me.(*To be honest, I am as irregular with mine to them).*

Therefore: I resolve to keep all my correspondence up to date.

"*I know better*" than to drive our car without putting gas in it. My husband has repeatedly explained to me, in his most gentle manner, that he doesn't care to run out of gas on his way to work in the morning.

Therefore: I resolve to keep gas in the car at all times.

"*I know better*" than to let my bank statements pile up in a drawer until my checkbook balance requires service charge subtractions each time I overdraw my account.

Therefore: I resolve to balance my bank statements promptly upon their arrival.

Here is a word of warning.

Mention to no one that this list exists. Immediately upon its completion, place it in an envelope, seal it, and promptly convert it to ashes and smoke.

Your ironing will continue to pile up, your corresponding friends will think of you warmly at Christmas time, your husband will get good exercise, the bank will feel that you accept and respect their bookkeeping procedures and your conscience will be free to glide into 1965 in friendly and familiar surroundings.

2022 and continuing......

It's been quite awhile since I've made a New Year's resolution.

Please don't think ill of me. I learned years ago that such an endeavor was a complete waste of my time.

Thank heaven for permanent press clothing that needs no ironing.

I remember the days when Grandma took my clothes needing ironing and sprinkled them with water, rolled them up, and put them in the freezer for me to iron later. I also learned something that may be of use to you.

If sprinkled clothes are stored in the freezer for two weeks or longer, they will be surprisingly damp when you thaw them. If the time is more than a week or two, your clothes may have to be sprinkled again.

(Grandma never approved of "re-sprinkling".)

While I'm thinking of it, thank heaven for the invention of the computer and emails. I am now able to respond within minutes to correspondence from my friends.

(Why didn't someone think of this before?)

I try to fill up the gas tank as soon as I see that there is a little space after *full*. The price of gas has reached an unthinkable $4.89 per gallon. When you fill the tank as soon as you've used a gallon or two, it doesn't cost as much.

(You can check that out, math was never my favorite subject.)

Although I require the bank to send printed statements to me, I also have my bank records on the computer. I let my printed statements recline unopened in a drawer. There is always the possibility of the computer being down. This would restrain me from checking my account online.

(In case of an electrical outage, the unopened, printed statements in the drawer may also come in handy.)

I do not recommend New Year's resolutions.

If you feel the need to put resolutions in writing, this is my advice.

Use a sealed and unmarked envelope. Destroy it as quickly as possible after January 1st. Fire is the most reliable solution.

(The envelope may also be thrown in the garbage but there is always the possibility someone could find it at the dump.)

Listen to your conscience.

MUSINGS OF A HOMEMAKER

By Mary Anne Tuck

1964

(Houghton Lake Resorter)

Houghton Lake, Michigan

(If your memory doesn't go back as far as 1964, you may want to get someone to help you read and interpret this.)

It should be of increasing concern to America at large that we are all becoming hopelessly addicted to the beckoning television networks.

I, for one, have resisted the temptation mightily.

The 21 inch screen which sits on the north side of our living room, holds little or no attraction for me.

Recently, I remarked to my husband, (as I left the breakfast table to eat with Hugh Downs' *"Today Show"* in the living room), *"Television is not interesting to me any more, not with my busy mornings."*

Later, as my young sons left for school, I noticed Mr. Green Jeans was showing *"Captain Kangaroo"* some baby chicks. A person might wonder if we are ruining our children's minds by letting them watch so much television. (The program was almost over, so I watched the rest of the Captain's program after the school bus picked up the kids.)

While clearing up the kitchen and absorbing the intricacies of *"American Government"* on our television screen, my thoughts strayed to carefree summer days when I could relax and watch the *"Detroit Tigers"* ball games, which are all televised.

After exercising with *"Ed Allen"* and enjoying my mid-morning coffee break with *"Lucy"*, it was time to turn off the television and turn on the radio for

"Pete and Gladys."

My kindergarten son was off to afternoon session when the *"CBS Midday News"* had finished. After lunch I took some time to watch my favorite serial, *"As The World Turns"*, which I've watched nearly every day for the past eight years.

(It's only half an hour. One could scarcely call that an addiction.)

The kids get home from school about twenty minutes after *"The Secret Storm"* and twenty minutes before *"News, Weather, and Sports"*. I plan to have supper on the stove so I can watch the forecast to see what tomorrow's weather will be.

On Monday night, my husband leaves for his bowling league just before *"The Donna Reed Show"*.

Tuesdays find me missing *"Mr. Novak"* and the *"Red Skelton Show"*, (but not by far), as I leave for my own bowling league at the local lanes.

We try to visit our folks on Wednesdays at five minutes to *"The Virginian"*, (they have color television and we haven't acquired one at this time.)

Thursdays, about a quarter to *"Dr. Kildare"*, I like to fix popcorn and soft drinks to spend a most enjoyable evening of relaxing with television.

Fridays bring evening grocery shopping.

By ten minutes to *"Jack Paar"* I'm ready to rest. The groceries are put away for another week.

On Saturday, of course, it's family night with our kids staying up until almost *"Saturday Night at the Movies"*. A good night's rest is needed so they won't be too tired to watch *"Walt Disney's Wonderful World of Color"* on Sunday evening.

I thoroughly believe in letting the young ones watch special programs of such high quality.

You know, now that I think about it, it's difficult to believe there are people in this world who get so wrapped up in television viewing they scarcely ever need to look at a clock.

I just cannot understand.....

2022

...not sure my viewing schedule has changed too much.

I have more choices and the screen is much larger.

Programs are many and I have more time to myself. The children have grown to adulthood and have homes of their own.

It's up to me to choose how to spend the hours in my day. There is more time to *spend* than I had in 1964.

With that in mind, the news is very interesting to me; the state of the world, and the government.

There is no longer need for eight hours of sleep so I plan to be in front of the television by 4:30 a.m. so I can watch the weather on our local channel.

Since I've DVR'd the *Gutfeld! Show* which is on after I've gone to bed at ten, I review it between 5 a.m and 6 a.m. while waiting for *Fox And Friends First* at six. Some folks probably don't know that when you DVR a program you can skip past the commercials. It's helpful and saves time.

(I've noticed that 8 clicks gets me right past a commercial on the *Gutfeld! Show.*)

I usually leave the television on the *Fox News* channel all day in case an event occurs and it will be broadcast first hand. Sometimes, however, I switch over to *Sirius XM* where *Willie's Road House* brings back sweet memories of the old days.

Occasionally, but not often, I switch to the *"Andy Griffith Show"* or *"The Golden Girls"*. They bring back some laughter. Sometimes a good laugh is relaxing.

When all of the above has filled me with as many political reports and sweet memories as I can handle, I can always return to ...

"The Music" and Willie.

Classic Country is my choice. Current country music doesn't hold an attraction for me. So I turn to Classic Country and find myself singing along with Merle, Loretta, Patti and Reba...the songs I remember.

You know the ones I'm talking about. I enjoy listening to the Statler Brothers singing *"Whatever Happened To Randolph Scott?"*

They say music is good for the soul and the body. I'm in a good place....

(By the way, what *did* happen to Randolph Scott?)

Guess I can always Google it.

1965
Musings

MUSINGS OF A HOMEMAKER
By Mary Anne Tuck
1965
(Houghton Lake Resorter)
Houghton Lake, Michigan

If you are standing in the great state of Michigan...
Celebrate!
Surely as the Robin is our state bird and the Apple Blossom our favorite
flower, Michigan is a wonderful state.
From the Mighty Mac to the Motor City, Michigan is filled with history,
industry, woods and waters; together they gladden the heart of the most
particular soul.
Although other states may lay claim to him, a proud Michigander can
regale you with true myths of the most fabulous of all Michigan native
residents, Paul Bunyan and his Mighty Blue Ox, Babe.
If it weren't for the great love this hearty lumberjack had for Babe, we
might never have know the beauty and majesty of the Great Lakes which
Paul made to provide a watering hole for Babe; or so the story goes.

Michigan easily claims the title of the most beautiful state in the union.
Her boundaries alone distinguish her from all the other states. None can
boast the shape of a mitten, surrounded on three sides by water. The
Upper Peninsula is separated from the Lower Peninsula by a body of
water called the Straits of Mackinac; joining the Upper and Lower
Peninsula with the engineering miracle of the mighty Mackinac Bridge.

Among Michigan's many other achievements, is the International Bridge,
which links the United States and Canada for the third time. The bridge
was built on the foundation of regard, respect and a persistent desire
between two of the most powerful nations in the world; Canada and the
United States of America, to promote an alliance based on
infinite goodwill.
The outline of the "thumb" area defines the mitten. Tourists are
delighted to find they can actually stand upon the pointed tip of the

"Thumb" nail, with the regal beauty of Lake Huron before them and the rock bound coast called Point Aux Barques nearby.
The ten million people who call Michigan home are glad they live in this great state; delighted to have had an entire week set aside for the sole purpose of proclaiming her beauty to the world.

If you seek a pleasant peninsula, look about you! You're in Michigan It's a great state!

Remembering 1965

It can't be, but here it is.
The end of another year and it was really such a short twelve months. We slipped from the grip of a frigid, snow-bound, Michigan winter into the youngest of spring times with scarcely a passing thought to the demise of another season.

Oh, how we looked forward to those precious summer days and nights with visions of outdoor get-togethers, shady picnics and lazy Sunday afternoons. While we were anticipating such stirring events, the warmth of a longed for summer trod cautiously by without our realizing what we looked forward to, was in reality, with us every passing moment.

With a start, we admitted it was time for the kids to go back to school, the summer residents to close their cottages, and the year around residents to relax a little. The usual peppering of duck blinds appeared as if by some pre-arranged signal, on the deep blue autumn waters of Houghton Lake. We began to realize, with a twinge, the holiday season was approaching preceded by the annual pursuit of small game and the elusive white-tail deer, just how elusive we didn't yet know in the early fall.

Now here we are, half-way through the holidays, making plans for a brand new year; winding up unfinished projects and anticipating the beginning of new ones.

Perhaps your "1965" held a smattering of regrets, much fulfillment, and a multitude of wishes not fulfilled; we hope so for it takes a little of all to create a good year. Without reservation, we all had a good year, in one way or another.

Let's see now, it's time for resolutions. We have to make a few even if they never get beyond the planning stage. We've had twelve months to consider the order of their importance.

Family first, we'll provide a little more understanding, and a lot more patience. Why should the twenty one years between the oldest son and me be so much farther apart than the thirty years between my parents and me? It seems we not only have a resolution but a thought to ponder in the coming twelve months.

Friends, try to be a better one. The giving always reaps more pleasure than the receiving and seems to make the receiving more deeply moving and personally rewarding.

If we resolve no more than two, we stand a very good chance of fifty percent success in following through.

The trite phrases come to mind...best wishes...good luck..may the New Year bring you happiness..may you truly enjoy each precious moment of every bright day of every wonderful month of the new year, 1966.

It's a most precious gift, twelve new months to savor and enjoy. Please do!

Recipes

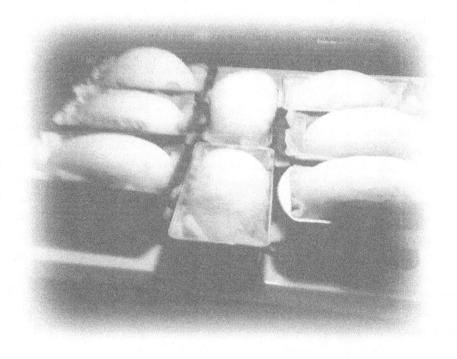

☑☛☞🖐✔☛☒ *FROM MY CUPBOARD*

Mary Anne's Healthy Homemade Bread

Homemade bread is my favorite.

While trying to find a way to make it so it wouldn't be fattening; I decided to check out the calories in the shortening to see if it could be replaced with unsweetened applesauce for less calories. *(For the moisture content.)*

The shortening was 1800 calories against 100 in the same amount of applesauce. *EUREKA!* All I needed to find out was how it would taste.

It tastes *WONDERFUL.*

There is no flavor of applesauce, just really good homemade bread.

This recipe makes 7-8 loaves; 7 would be best but you could make each loaf a bit smaller and come up with 8.

I freeze mine.

Hope you take the time to try it. It takes the better part of a day to make a batch of bread, but you'll feel so good about yourself, it will be well worth the effort.

(The compliments are nice too.)

1/4 cup yeast, 2 tblsp sugar, 2 1/2 cups very warm (not hot) water. Mix it well.

Let stand for at least ten minutes to get the yeast working. It will be just fine when you get ready to add it even if it's more than 10 minutes

2 1/2 cups scalded milk *(put the pan over a low burner until slight skim forms on top)* Use regular milk or evaporated. Let the milk cool to warm.

(Sometimes I place the pan in a larger pan with a couple of inches of cold water in the bottom to get the milk cooled down.)

1 cup *UNSWEETENED* applesauce, 1 cup white sugar, 1 1/2 tblsp salt..mix well

Add milk and yeast mixture to applesauce and sugar and salt

Mix thoroughly with large mixer

I use a large Kitchen Aid Mixer..I've had my mixer since 1983 and I've never had a bit of trouble with it. Don't know if they make equipment to last that long anymore.

7 eggs beaten *(add to liquid last)*..mix well

Add 5 lb flour, mixing slowly, but well, after each addition.

I prefer King Arthur Bread Flour. *(5 pound bags plus a little regular flour if the "King" isn't quite enough)*

Roll out dough on *WELL* floured board or counter. *My mixer isn't large enough to completely mix the amount of flour needed.* The remainder will be added as you knead the dough. *(You'll know the texture is right when you see it.)*

Place in greased pan...*you'll need a large one.* Let rise until doubled in bulk. About 1 1/2 to 2 hours. *(Cover dough with clean cloth as it rises. I let mine sit on top of my stove and turn the oven on to about 200 to make a warm place.)*

Punch down and let it rest for 10 minutes

Form the dough into a long round piece and cut the 7 or 8 sections for the loaves. *(You'll figure it out.)*
Knead each section and form the loaf.

You'll need bread pans according to your number. *(Of course)*

I've found that using Parchment paper is the best lining for the pans. It keeps the sides from sticking and pops right off when the bread is finished;. using a spray can with shortening to put a little on the tops of the loaves before baking them. Sometimes it makes the tops look wrinkly when they're done baking. It's up to you. Do it..or don't do it. The bread will be good either way.

(Again, I lay a cloth lightly over the loaves as they raise in the pans.)

Let the loaves raise for 1 1/2 hours or until doubled in bulk.

Bake at 395 deg. for 25-30 minutes. *When they look right, you'll know it.*

I use a 2 gallon freezer bag for one loaf.
There isn't enough room for 2 loaves but a 1 gallon freezer bag isn't large enough.
Save the bags for next time.
You're going to want to bake this bread often.

* * *

Louise Allen's Coffee Cake Ring

Why is it food always tastes better at the farm?

The day we entered the kitchen of Louise Allen, the tantalizing aroma of baking cinnamon bread met us at the door. A cup of coffee, freshly baked coffee cake and the friendly conversation of Louise and her family will always be remembered.

We were searching for a home to buy.

The Allen family made us feel as though this twenty acre farm was the answer to our quest. That happened sixty four years ago; we still live at Hidden Meadows Farm and seeing this recipe written in my book brings back pleasant memories.

1 Cup Milk

3 Tblsp Butter

3 Heaping Tblsp Sugar

3/4 tsp Salt (or 1/2)

2 1/4 tsp Dry Yeast

1 Egg - Beaten

1 1/2 tsp Vanilla (or Lemon flavoring)

Heat milk to warm. Add butter, sugar, salt, yeast. Add egg & vanilla. Add flour until it feels like Bisquick dough. *(You'll know when it's just right)*

Turn out on floured board & kneed til smooth.

Let raise til double in bulk.

Roll out. Spread with melted butter and cinnamon, brown sugar, raisins if desired, and nuts.

Roll up and form in a ring. Place on cookie sheet.

Bake at 325 deg. 20-25 minutes.

This is how Louise gave the recipe to me. Hope you enjoy it!

Mom's Chocolate Cake
Heavenly

Mother's Day is every day to me. My Mother was a registered nurse and a wonderful cook. Friends and family enjoyed her company. A smile and laughter were always with her as well as her funny jokes. Everyone enjoyed them too, almost as much as her cooking.

Time passes, memories stay with us.

INGREDIENTS

2 cups cake flour

1/2 tsp salt

1 tsp vanilla

1 tsp soda

1 tsp vinegar

1/2 cup shortening

1 1/2 cups sugar

2 eggs

1 cup sour milk

2 squares bitter chocolate

* * *

Sift and measure flour. Add salt and sift 3 times. Cream shortening, add sugar and one egg (unbeaten).

Mix well - add another egg & beat 2 minutes.

(The Egg And You...)

To test the age of an egg, place in deep pan of cold water. If it lies on its side, it is fresh. If it stands at an angle, it is probably 3-4 days old. If it stands on end upright, it is over 10 days old. If it floats to the top...get rid of it!

Add vanilla, flour and sour milk.

Add melted chocolate and mix.

Lastly, dissolve soda in vinegar and add to batter. Beat a few seconds.

Bake for 30 minutes (or more) in 350 deg. oven. (11x13 Pan)

* * *

Icing

2 cups powdered sugar

1 sq. chocolate

3 tbsp butter

6 tbsp cream

1/4 tsp Black Walnut Extract

1/2 cup nutmeats

Dissolve chocolate and butter in double boiler.

Add other ingredients and beat until creamy

* * *

Johnny Hoosier Cake

This recipe is in my mother's handwriting, so apparently her blessing is upon it. I've never used it, but it reads well. Maybe you should try it.

Sift into bowl..2 cups flour, 1 tsp. soda, 2 cups sugar.

Melt 2 sticks margarine

Add 4 tblsp cocoa & 1 cup water.

Bring to rapid boil. *Pour* over dry ingredients.

Add 1 cup buttermilk, 2 eggs, 1 tsp. vanilla.

Mix well.

Bake in jelly roll pan @ 350 deg...15 or 20 minutes until done.

(Cake will be moist.)

ICING

Melt 1 stick margarine. *Add* 4 tblsp cocoa, 6 tblsp buttermilk. *Bring* to boil

Add 1 lb. powdered sugar, 1 tsp. Vanilla, 1 cup nutmeats & *beat.*

(Reflecting on the margarine; Mother was using the recipe in the 40's...try butter)

That's about it!

* * *

Delicious Lemon Pudding Cake

I don't know who shared this wonderful recipe and note. Even so, I like her. It's written on plain note paper by hand. Hope you love her too, whoever she may be.

4 Eggs

1 lb 3 oz Yellow Cake Mix (not deluxe)

1 Pkg Instant Lemon Pudding

3/4 C. Corn Oil

3/4 Cup Water

1/4 tsp Grated lemon or orange peel

Beat eggs, add all ingredients & blend well.

Bake on bottom shelf in tube pan. Turn out on rack & dust with

powdered sugar. Bake at 350 deg. 40-45 min.

******

(this is a very good but not sickeningly rich frosting.)

Sander's Frosting

1/2 C. Crisco

1/2 Cup Butter

1 Cup Sugar

3 tsp Vanilla

1/2 Cup Hot Milk

1 Egg White

Mix well add hot milk to beaten egg white then combine all ingredients & beat till frothy. Coconut may be sprinkled over top of frosting or shaved semi sweet choc is very nice.

I have used the Deluxe package for the Lemon Cake & it turns out o.k. too although the plain package seems a little lighter textured cake.

This frosting keeps nicely for several days....providing the cake lasts that long. Ha!

Crunchy Rhubarb Cake

This one is written in longhand on a piece of paper.

There's no name so I can't give credit to anyone. I'm going to post it

just as it's written.

Cream 1 1/2 cup sugar & 1/2 cup shortening. Add 1 egg & beat. Mix in 1 cup sour cream or buttermilk, 2 cups flour, 1 tsp. soda, 1/4 tsp. salt, 1/2 tsp vanilla. Add 2 cups diced rhubarb to batter. Mix well. Pour batter into a 9 x 13 greased pan. Combine 1/2 cup sugar, 2 tsp. cinn. Sprinkle over batter. Bake at 350 deg for 30 min

I haven't made this myself. But if it tastes as good as it sounds, even if you just read the title, we both ought to try it.

* * *

Apple Brownies
MMM..Sounds Good Enough To Eat

Another recipe from "Toots", my Mother's friend, who also happened to be a registered nurse. She was not only a great nurse, but also a good cook. This recipe in her handwriting says, "it's good". I believe her.

Cream 1/2 cup melted oleo with 1 cup sugar.

Add one egg.

Sift 1 cup flour, 1/tsp baking powder, 1/2 tsp soda, 1/4 tsp salt, 1 tsp cinnamon.

Add to cream mix and mix well.

Stir in 3 medium apples peeled & sliced thin & 1/2 cup nuts.

Place in 9x9 pan-greased.

Bake @ 350 deg. 40-45 minutes.

"Will be moist & good"

Mrs. Quickel's Baked Cranberries

Florence Quickel and her husband were friends of my parents when I was a young girl; (*Mr.* and *Mrs.* Quickel to my sister and me when we were children.)

I remember going to their home on a little lake called Ambrose Lake north of the town where I grew up; West Branch, Michigan.

The handwritten letter that contained four recipes and a note to my Mother was apparently written at or near the time of the assassination of John F. Kennedy.

Be sure and read her note to my Mother at the end of the recipe for Apricot Squares. Hope you take the time to read it. I will record her recipes and notes just as she has written them.

****

In a shallow pan place 1 lb Cranberries, 2 1/4 C. sugar. Place in oven about 375 deg. & bake till soft. (*watch carefully*)

Take shallow small pan & take 1 tblsp creamery butter & toast 1 cup broken pieces of walnuts. (this can be done in oven at same time you bake cran.) *This needs watching because it will burn very quickly.*

When cran. are cooked, add the nuts, 1 cup orange marmalade, juice of 1 lemon.

* * *

Mrs. Quickel's Apricot Squares

The short letter that Mrs. Quickel wrote is attached at the end of this recipe. I found it interesting.

6 cups flour

2 tblsp sugar

3 beaten eggs

1/2 tsp salt

1 lb lard (shortening?)

1 yeast cake

3/4 cup scalded milk cooled to luke warm

Combine flour, lard, sugar & salt blended as for pie crust. Dissolve yeast in warm milk, add to first mixture. Add eggs & knead to a smooth dough Refrigerate over night in covered bowl.

Next..cover pie board with 1/4 cup sugar. Roll dough on sugar about 1/4 in. thick or a little thinner. Cut into 2 1/2 in. squares.

Into each square place 1/2 tsp apricot or any desired paste & fold up corners into a peak & pin with tooth picks.

Bake 15 min in 375 deg. oven. Remove tooth picks while warm. Picks can be reused.

Her observations..

"We like cooked seasoned dried apricots best in these squares. However, dried peaches or any jam is good. I'm going to try Baked Cranberries this year in the squares. The Apricot just seems to go so well with the sugared dough. We feel that ordinary jam is just too sweet.

I thought the Baked Cranberry with less sugar would be tart too, like apricots. It's surprising how well you can pin in these squares for as soft as the dough is. Of course, a few pop open during baking that's why the paste should be sort of thick. This paste can be bought in cans too but again, we like the cooked dried apricots sweet taste.

Continuing with Mrs. Quickel's short letter....

Hi...I'm sort of pushing the cart instead of pulling it. Ha. I thought I would only have a few min to write the recipes & I wanted you to have them before Christmas.

12

We came home yesterday (Monday) noon & we can't seem to get into the groove. Things sure happened since we saw you.

One wonders how much wickedness we must endure. While it's a tremendous burden for the Kennedy children I keep thinking of the Oswald children. They can never live down this tragic episode. I'm glad they live in the land of opportunity where if they lived in Russia they might be sent to Siberia.

Several Clear Lake men died last week also. A Mr. Nofsinger who had the L&M Market there next to the Beer Garden. The other man was Fred Miller. They used to have Shaw's old cabins & gas station.

Well, I've got a few more things to put away etc. Here's hoping you have a nice Holiday season.

Sure was nice visiting with you folks. Hope we didn't detain you too much.

Lovingly....Quickel

* * *

This note brings back memories of times when my Mother would receive a letter from her brothers in Illinois. It was usually a four page letter and required her to take some time, sit down and read, and find out what the family was doing.

Now we have the internet. It doesn't have that same homey quality, does it?

Just remembering yesterday...again.

* * *

Delectable Chocolate Chip Cookies w Rice Krispies

You're on your own here. Doesn't sound difficult, let me know how it turns out.

Beat until well blended (the following);

1 cup Oleo

3/4 cup White Sugar

3/4 cup Brown Sugar

Add 2 Eggs, 1 tsp Vanilla/Beat well

Add dry ingredients and mix.

Stir in 2 cups Rice Krispies and 1 cup chocolate morsels.

Drop by level tblsp on greased baking sheet

Bake @ 350 deg - 10 minutes or until lightly browned

Cool 1 minute..then remove to wire racks

Makes 6 dozen 2 1/2" cookies

* * *

Brer Rabbit Gingers

Yields 8 dozen

2 Cups Molasses

1 Cup Sugar

2 T Cider Vinegar

2 T Ginger

1/4 t Nutmeg

4 t Soda

1 Cup Shortening

1 Egg

7 Cups Flour

1 1/2 t Cinnamon

1 t Salt

Cream together shortening, sugar. Add egg, beat well. Add molasses and vinegar. Sift together flour, spices, soda, and salt. Add to creamed mixture. Add 1 cup boiling water. Mix well. If necessary add more flour to make a soft dough. Drop by teaspoons on greased baking sheet. Bake in moderate oven @ 350 degrees 10-12 minutes.

A friend of many years, named Fran, gave me this recipe. I recall that the cookies are good.
Fran was a bowling buddy of mine.
Those were the days. Yes, they were!

* * *

Mary's Cowboy Cookies

What is it about the cowboy scenario that speaks to us from the days when we went to the movies on Saturday afternoon to see Roy Rogers, Gene Autry and of course, Randolph Scott? As I recall, the price of admission at our local theater was 35 cents.

We listened to The Lone Ranger on the radio and can't seem to get "Hi-Ho Silver...Awayyyyyyy....out of our memories.

My friend Mary shared her "Cowboy" cookie recipe with me and now I'll share it with you.

1 Cup Butter

1 Cup Sugar (White)

1 Cup Brown Sugar

2 Eggs

2 Cups Flour

1/2 t. Salt

1 t. Baking Soda

1 t. Baking Powder

1 t. Vanilla

2 1/2 Cups Oatmeal

1 Cup Chips (Chocolate or any flavor)

1 Cup Rice Crispies

Cream together butter and sugars. Beat in eggs. Add flour, salt, soda, baking powder and mix well.
Stir in vanilla, oatmeal, chips and crispies.
Drop by teaspoonful onto ungreased cookie sheet.
Bake at 350 deg. for 10 minutes.

* * *

Lucille's Heavenly Coconut Cherry Bars

One Cup Unsifted Flour

1/2 Cup Softened Margarine

3 Tbsp Sugar

* * *

Combine 1 Cup flour with margarine & 3 tbsp sugar.

Blend well.

Press firmly in bottom of 9" square pan.

Bake 350 Deg. for 25 minutes.

Mix Together

1/4 cup flour

1/2 tsp. baking powder

1/4 tsp salt

Gradually add

3/4 cup sugar

2 eggs slightly beaten

1 tsp vanilla

Add sugar to eggs and beat well. Add vanilla.

1 1/3 Angel Flake Coconut

1/2 cup chopped maraschino cherries

1/4 cup chopped nuts

Add to flour mixture and stir well.

Stir in coconut, cherries and nuts.

Spread over baked crust. Bake 35 minutes longer. Cut into bars while still warm.

Makes 24 bars.

Stella's Date Pinwheel Cookies - Top of the Line

My favorite cookies. Takes a bit of time but they're worth every moment you spend making them. The right to be called;

"The Cadillac Of Cookies."

FILLING

2 1/4 Cups pitted chopped dates

1 cup sugar

1 cup water

1 cup chopped nuts

(Boil slowly 10 minutes, mixing constantly.. let cool until warm)

MIX TOGETHER

1 cup shortening

2 cups brown sugar

3 eggs (beaten)

4 cups sifted flour

1/2 tsp salt

1/2 tsp soda

Roll out dough on floured surface about 3/8" thick. Spread thickened filling on it.

Roll up into roll and wrap with waxed paper. Refrigerate several hours or until firm enough to slice. (Approximately 1/4 inch thick)

Bake 10-12 minutes at 400 deg.

* * *

Caramel Layer Chocolate Chip Squares

My recipe paper shows the date October 13, 1986. A pre-printed caption at the top says *JUST A NOTE FROM...TOOTS*.

Everyone called my Mother's friend, "Toots". As I recall, her name was Violet although not many folks knew that. She was a registered nurse, as was my Mother, and they worked together for years and were best friends.

Toots was a wonderful cook. If the recipe has her name on it, and this one does, then I know it's a good one. Hope it turns out well for you. *(I'm writing it exactly as Toots wrote it.)*

Mix pkg caramels with 1/3 C. evap. milk. Heat until caramels are melted. Melt 1//2 C. (or little more) of oleo. Mix pkg. German Choc cake mix, melted oleo and 1/3 C. canned milk & 1 C. chopped nuts by hand until dough sticks to-gether. Grease & flour 9x13 pan. Place 1/2 of cake mix on bottom of pan. Bake @ 350 Deg. for 6 min.

Sprinkle 1 C. choc chips over baked crust. Spread caramel mixture over choc. chips. Crumble remaining cake mixture over caramel mix.

Bake 350 Deg 15-18 min. Cool slightly. Refrigerate 30 min. to set caramel mixture. Cut into squares.

I've never tried making this recipe. But, I just gained 10 pounds while I was typing it out.

* * *

Tim's Chocolate Chip Cookies

During the later years of his life, our son Tim enjoyed baking. One of his favorite recipes was for chocolate chip cookies.. He gave the recipe to me over the phone, so every time I look at this insignificant piece of paper where I jotted it down, I remember the joy of hearing him talk about his great cookies.

(Memories really are wonderful, don't you think?)

1 Cup Soft Butter

1 Cup White Sugar

1 Cup Brown Sugar (Packed)

2 Eggs

2 tsp Vanilla

3 Cups Flour

1 tsp Baking Soda

2 tsp Hot Water

1/2 tsp Salt

2 Cups Chocolate Chips

Bake in 350 deg oven - 10 minutes approximately

Yields 4 dozen

* * *

Popular Fruit Punch Bars

My recipe note says *FROM THE DESK OF TOOTS DENIO*...So Toots must have loved these delightful snack recipes. *(There are more from "Toots" my Mother's friend.)*

We love them too!

2 Eggs

1 1/2 C. Sugar

1 lb.1 oz. Can of Fruit Cocktail

2 1/2 C. Flour

1 1/2 tsp. Soda

1/2 tsp. Salt

1 tsp. Vanilla

1 1/3 C. Coconut

1/2 C. Chopped nuts

Grease & flour 15 x 10 jelly roll pan. Beat eggs & sugar at high speed till light & fluffy. Add fruit, flour & soda, salt & vanilla. Beat at med. speed till mixed. Scrape side of bowl. Spread in pan.

Bake @ 350 deg. for 20-25 minutes until brown

Glaze

3/4 C. Sugar

1/2 C. Butter

1/4 C. Evaporated Milk

1/2 tsp. Vanilla

COMBINE

****

Bring to boil. Boil 2 minutes stirring constantly. Pour over bars. Put coconut and chopped nuts on top.

Tender Chicken & Rice Casserole

This little recipe is written on a piece of note paper, all ragged around the edges as if it's been handled a bit. However, it's in my Mother's handwriting, so I know it's a good one.

1   7 oz pkg Minute Rice

1   Can Cream of Mushroom Soup

1 Can Cream of Chicken Soup

1 Can Milk (soup can)

Mix together & pour into 9x13 dish.

Over the top, lay pieces of uncooked chicken.   Sprinkle 1 pkg. dried onion soup mix over the chicken.

Cover with aluminum foil & seal the edges.

Bake 2 hours @ 350 Deg.

Home Style Noodle Bake - A Casserole

Cook and drain 2 1/2 cup fine noodles.

Add...

1 Cup Cream style Cottage Cheese

1 Cup Dairy Sour Cream

1/4 Cup finely chopped onions

1 clove garlic (minced)

1 tblsp Soy Sauce

1 tblsp Poppy Seeds

Put in casserole.   Sprinkle with Paprika and Parmesan Cheese

Bake 30 minutes at 350 Deg.

Lorrayne's Delightful Breakfast Casserole

Lorrayne always fixed this delightful breakfast for the Easter season Maundy Thursday breakfast at our church. Of course, she had to increase the amount of the ingredients, for there were always many ladies in attendance. It tasted so good, and there was always enough for second helpings.

1 1/2 lb Hash browns (2lb)

1/2 lb Ham or Sausage (1lb)

2 Onions (4)

Green Peppers (Your choice)

1 1/4 Cup Shredded Sharp Cheese

2 Cups Milk

1 Can Cream of Mushroom Soup

4 Eggs (Beaten)

1 tsp Dry Mustard (ground)

1/4 tsp Pepper

Place ingredients in greased pan. (hash browns, meat, onion, green peppers, cheese)

Combine eggs, milk, mustard and pepper/Pour over ingredients in pan.

Cover and refrigerate overnight. Remove 30 minutes before baking.

Bake at 350deg. covered for 15 minutes. Bake uncovered one hour, 'til knife comes out clean. Let stand 10 - 15 minutes before serving.

Cowboy Surprise Breakfast Casserole
Easy and Good

This is a great dish for breakfast for several people. We were attending a rodeo twenty years ago....

at "Cow Camp" south of McBain, Michigan. We spent the week-end in our 5th wheel, along with our grandson who was interested in bull-riding... Misjudging the oven in the camper and its ability to produce, I waited and waited and waited, and the casserole wasn't done. Finally, it was ready. My grandson commented, "We could just call this "Cowboy Surprise"...and so we do...

every year on Christmas morning for our family breakfast..

2 packages shredded potatoes

1 onion-shredded

1 green pepper-shredded

2 dozen scrambled eggs

1 tsp salt

1/2 tsp pepper

2 lb chopped, cooked bacon/or sausage/or ham

Mix together, bake in LARGE oblong cake pan. Line pan with aluminum or parchment paper for easier cleanup.

450 Degrees 45 minutes Serves 10...

Scrambled eggs tend to continue cooking after removal from the oven..don't wait until they look finished or they'll be dry.

Good luck with your Cowboy Surprise. It's pretty tasty. And...the memories get better every year.

Mother's Macaroni And Cheese

One of my Mother's favorite casserole recipes. She had many. Written in pencil on the back of a place mat, it's in her handwriting. Seeing her handwriting is precious to me. It isn't fancy, but it's good if my Mother is sharing it.

8 oz   Macaroni

3 T   Oleo

2 C   Milk

2 T   Cornstarch or flour

1/4 C   Grated Onion

1/2 t Dry Mustard

1/4 t Worcestershire Sauce

1/4 t Salt

1/8 t Pepper

8 oz   Grated Cheddar Cheese

Cook macaroni. Drain and place in buttered 2 qt casserole.. In sauce pan melt butter, saute onion, stir in flour.   Slowly add milk until thickened. Add spices, cheese, stir until melted. Pour over macaroni, sprinkle with crumbs.   Bake at 350 deg 30-40 minutes. *(She didn't say what kind of crumbs. You'll have to figure that out for yourself.)*

Yummy Strawberry Dessert

If this tastes as good as the ingredients sound, we should have a remarkable offering for family and friends. Let's go!

2 10oz pkgs frozen strawberries

1 can crushed pineapple (drained)

3 mashed bananas

1 cup chopped pecans (nuts)

1 small pkg strawberry jello

1 cup boiling water

1 large carton sour cream

Dissolve jello in water, stir in strawberries, bananas, pineapple & nuts. Pour half into dish and refrigerate. When set, spread sour cream over top. Then add the rest of the jello. Refrigerate again.

Hmm...sounds simple. Let's try it!

Ella's Cherry Cheese Dessert

Ella was a great cook!
She was as organized in her baking as she was in her life. Like a
sister to me, Ella came to live with our family in 1939. I was
four and she was eighteen. She became a country school
teacher in the 1940's; wife mother, grandmother.
Her recipes are worth trying.

If this tastes as good as the ingredients sound, we should have a remarkable offering for family and friends. Let's go!

2 10oz pkgs frozen strawberries

1 can crushed pineapple (drained)

3 mashed bananas

1 cup chopped pecans (nuts)

1 small pkg strawberry jello

1 cup boiling water

1 large carton sour cream

Dissolve jello in water, stir in strawberries, bananas, pineapple & nuts. Pour half into dish and refrigerate. When set, spread sour cream over top. Then add the rest of the jello. Refrigerate again.

Hmm...sounds simple. Try it!

Cool and Unusual Coconut Dessert

Sounds good to me!

CRUST

1 cup flour

1/2 cup oleo

1/2 cup pecans (chopped)

1/3 to 1/2 cup crushed corn flakes

2 tbsp sugar

Mix and press into a 9 x 13 pan. Bake at 375deg for 12-15 minutes

TOPPING

1 8oz pkg Philadelphia cream cheese

1 Cup powdered Sugar

1 Cup Cool Whip

* * *

Cream the cream cheese. Add powdered sugar and fold in the Cool Whip. Spread on the crust. Over this spread cool custard, made as follows; Prepare 2 pkg coconut cream pudding mix using only 3 cups milk. Cool. Top with remaining Cool Whip. Sprinkle with Toasted Coconut and refrigerate.

(Toast the coconut while baking the crust.)

That's about it. Hope you like it!

Mrs. Quickel's Orange Fluff Pie

Do just as she says, and everything should come out just right.

1 can frozen Orange juice.
Add 1 can cold water,
1/2 cup sugar.
Heat to near boiling point.
Pour over 1 pkg lemon Jello.
Let this partly set.
Add 1 can (tall) chilled Carnation Milk (whipped).
Fold whipped milk gently into partly set Jello.
Pour into baked pie shell & place in refrig for a few hours to set up.

Amazing Coconut Pie

If it wasn't for recognizing her handwriting, I wouldn't know which recipes were from Mother or someone else. This one is hers. Did I tell you she was a great cook? Mother was a registered nurse. When she was at work, Grandma Matteson (her Mother) did the cooking. I'll have more of Grandma's recipes later. Stay tuned.

2 C Milk

3/4 C White Sugar

1/2 Cup biscuit mix

4 Eggs

1/4 C Oleo

1 1/2 t vanilla

1 C Baker Angel Flake Coconut

Combine first four ingredients in electric blender. Cover and blend on low speed 3 minutes. Pour into greased 9 inch pie pan. Let stand 5 minutes then sprinkle with coconut. Bake 350 deg. for 40 minutes. Serve warm or cool.

Mack's Plum Pudding

Not sure who Mack might be, but his recipe found its way into my recipe collection.   Sounds simple and quick. Just a thought though, I really wouldn't wait until the last minute to try it. You can always make it again for a special holiday.

INGREDIENTS

1 small lemon jello

1/2 tsp Cinnamon

1/4 tsp Cloves

3/4 Cup Ground Raisins

3/4 Cup Ground Dates

3/4 Cup Grape Nuts cereal

3/4 Cup Chopped Nuts

Make jello using "boiling" water

Add cinnamon & cloves & cool slightly

Grind raisins & dates & add to above & mix well

Stir in Grapenuts cereal & mix well

Cool slightly so nuts will not soften & add nut meats.

Set overnight.

Serve with whipped cream or ice-cream

Beef Salad

My friend, Dixie, is helping me out with recipes. It all sounds so good and I can't wait to try them.

BEEF SALAD

Ingredients:

1/2 cup sour cream

2 round tbsp. prepared horseradish

1/2 Lemon, *juiced*

2 tsp. Worcestershire sauce

Handful of chives, *finely chopped*

Handful of dill, *finely chopped*

1 1/2 tsp. coarse black pepper

1 pound deli roast beef, *(leftover, roast, pot roast or steaks)*

Watercress or arugula to serve

Gather your ingredients in a mixing bowl. Combine sour cream, horseradish, lemon juice, Worcestershire sauce, chives, dill and black pepper.

Chop the beef and combine with sauce.

When serving, arrange watercress or arugula *under and/or around* rounded scoops of the salad. *About 4 ounces per platter.*

Deviled Ham Salad

DEVILED HAM

1 pound deli ham sliced *(cooked ham)*

2 small ribs celery *with leafy tops*

1/2 red onion

2 cloves garlic

2 tbsp. thyme

1 tbsp. cayenne pepper sauce, *(more to taste)*

1 tbsp. Worcestershire sauce

Approximately 2 round tbsp. yellow mustard

3 tbsp. pickle relish

(Romaine or Bibb lettuce to serve)

Cut ham into coarse pieces. Place in food processor and finely chop by pulsing it 10-12 times. *Add to a mixing bowl .. return processor bowl to base.* Coarsely chop celery and onion, crush garlic, finely chop thyme, add to ham.

Season ham with cayenne pepper sauce, Worcestershire sauce, mustard and relish. Stir salad with spatula..

Rinse processor blade and bowl and return to base. To serve, arrange a small bed of lettuce leaves under rounded scoops of deviled ham, about 4 ounces per portion.

Chicken Salad

CHICKEN SALAD

1 pound cooked rotisserie chicken PLUS   all the fat and drippings from its container

2 small ribs celery

1 large shallot

1 large clove garlic, crushed

4 sprigs tarragon

salt and pepper

1/2 lemon

2 round tbsp Dijon mustard

Romaine or Bibb lettuce

About 2 tbsp small capers

Chopped cornichons serving

Separate the skin and bones from chicken and place meat in food processor with fat.   Pulse the processor to finely chop the chicken and transfer to a mixing bowl. Add processor bowl back to base, coarsely chop the celery, shallot, crushed garlic and tarragon leaves and pulse to finely chop.   Add to the chicken and season with salt and pepper.   Add lemon juice and mustard and stir well with rubber spatula. To serve, arrange the chicken salad on a bed of a few leaves of lettuce and top with capers and chopped cornichons.

To Serve

Cut edges of bread, arrange the bread on a baking sheet and lightly toast on both sides under broiler.   Cut toast from corner to corner.   Quarter eggs lengthwise. Cut cheese into portions.

Arrange platter: ham salad, hard-boiled eggs, beef salad, portion of cheese or cheeses of choice, chicken salad, 4 toast points per person.

Cauliflower Salad

Written on a piece of note paper and in my Mother's handwriting. I always trust Mother not to lead me astray. Let's try this one.

1 Head Cauliflower

1/4 Cup grated onion

1/2 Cup Miracle Whip Salad Dressing

8 oz pkg Cream Cheese

Whip onion, salad dressing & cheese until it coats cauliflower & carrots. Let refrigerate overnight.

Let me know how you like this. Sounds interesting. Looks to me like the cream cheese will make the difference.

Elegant Fruit Salad - A Favorite Dish

Another note from one of my favorite recipe sharers...(is that a word?)

She writes.............

"This fruit salad is quite a favorite dish. I forgot to say that the oranges and pineapples should be drained somewhat as it would become too sloppy. To be at its best the sour cream dressing should not be too thin. I have found that if I don't tell people it's sour cream dressing they eat it & really like it. When I tell them what it is they don't believe it. I'm going to try that cottage cheese salad recipe you gave me one of these week-ends when we have guests."

1 can Mandarin orange sections

1 can tidbit pineapple

3/4 cup coconut

1/2 cup nut meats (preferably pecans)

3/4 cup commercial sour cream.

Mix & let stand several hours before serving.

Wholesome Cottage Cheese Jello Salad

*This is the one the lady who gave us the Fruit Salad, was speaking about.
She said she was going to try it someday when she had guests. Remember
that? This is a wonderful salad for guests and also for family. It looks
pretty too!*

1 pkg Lemon Jello regular size

1 pkg lime Jello regular size

1 Cup Hot water

Mix thoroughly

* * *

1 Cup Salad Dressing (not mayonnaise)

1 regular size pkg Cottage Cheese small curd. (not small pkg and not
large)

Mix together with Jello/hot water - mix well - Place in refrigerator until set

Meanwhile

1 Green Pepper Ground

1 Small Onion Ground

3 Medium size Carrots Ground

Now

*When Jello mixture you've put in the refrigerator is set, beat it with a
mixer until it looks beaten. Add ground vegetables. Mix thoroughly.
Place in refrigerator until ready to eat. If you shake it and it just sits
there..it's ready.*

VANESSA'S PRETZEL SALAD

Vanessa was a long time friend of my parent's family. She and her husband, a pastor, built the log cottage at Lake Louise, North of Gaylord, Michigan, which my parents purchased and enjoyed for 25 years..a lovely lady and a good cook.... (must have been all those church dinners.)

2 1/2 cups Crushed Pretzels-3 3/4 tblsp Sugar-2 sticks margarine melted

Mix together. Press into 9 x 13 pan. Bake at 400 deg. for 8 minutes...COOL

8 Oz Cream Cheese- 1 cup sugar-1 8oz Cool Whip

Beat cream cheese with sugar at high speed 'til creamy. Fold in Cool Whip. Spread over first layer.

1 6 oz Strawberry Jello - 2 1/2 cup boiling water-10 or 20 oz frozen strawberries- dissolve jello in water-add frozen strawberries *(strawberries should thicken jello)* Chill 1/2 hour-pour over 2nd layer-refrigerate until set

Mrs. Quickel's Carrot Relish

This one is short and sweet. Sounds good though. No excuse for not trying it.

8 standard size carrots (coarsely grated)

1 cup sugar,

1 lemon juice & grated rind

I use that grater that forms a sort of long thin sliver.

(Told you it was short.)

Jeanette's Perfect Veggie Pizza

When the next door neighbor is a good friend and a good cook, you've got it made.

2 pkg Crescent rolls (Unroll & line jelly roll pan.)Bake at 350 deg.

8 - 12 minutes. Press gently if puffed up.

Mix together

1 # Cream cheese

1/2 Cup Mayonnaise

1/2 Cup Sour Cream

1 envelope Hidden Valley Ranch Dressing

Spread on Crust

Chop Fine 1/2 Cup each of the following;

Cauliflower, Broccoli, Carrots, Green Pepper, Green Onions, (Tomato & Mushroom if desired)

Mix the above vegetables together and sprinkle over the top

Sprinkle 3/4 to 1 Cup sharp grated cheddar cheese over top.

Evelyn's Classic Beef Jerky

This recipe card is dated December 10, 1989. Aunt Evelyn was a farmer's wife and a good cook. I haven't tried this Beef Jerky but here's the recipe for you just in case your man loves this stuff as much as mine does.

3-5 lbs very lean round steak

1 tsp onion powder

1/2 tsp black pepper

2 TBLSP liquid smoke

1 TBLSP salt

1 tsp garlic powder

A1 sauce...a little bit

1 cup warm water..mix together

Slice beef into strips 1/4 " thick 1/2" wide and about 4-5 " long. Roll it thin with a rolling pin. Cut across grain of meat for crisp jerky.

Marinate in covered container several hours or overnight. Drain and pat dry w/paper toweling. Heat dry (about 175 deg) until it gets crispy according to your wishes. (Check it often) Seal in plastic bags.

Grandma Matteson's Perfect Pickle Relish

2 Qt Cucumbers - Peeled and Ground

2 Qt Green Tomatoes - Ground

18 Onions - Ground

Add 1/3 cup salt - Mix

Let stand overnight

Drain

2 Bunches of Celery - cut fine or ground

3 Red Sweet Peppers - Chopped

8 Green Peppers - Chopped

1 TBLSP Celery Seed

1 TBLSP Mustard Seed

5 Cups White Sugar

1 1/2 Qt Vinegar

Mix together Cook 1 hour

Can while hot

A little green food coloring makes a difference in how it looks

Makes 10-14 Pints

Rum Balls....Mmmm

Haven't made these in a long, long time. My recipe dates back to the forties. Might be just what you'd like to try. Let me know how it works out for you.

1/2 lb. Vanilla Wafers

1 Cup pwd. Sugar

2 TBLSP Cocoa

1 Cup finely chopped nuts (preferably pecans)

1/2 Cup Light Corn Syrup

1/4 Cup Rum

DIRECTIONS

Roll wafers into very fine crumbs. Mix with cup of pwd. sugar & cocoa. Add chopped nuts, syrup, and rum. Stir until blended with a stiff texture. Shape into 1 inch balls. Let stand 1 hour and roll in pwd. sugar and put nut on top. Put sugar on hands when shaping balls.

Keep in tightly closed can for three days before using.

What's Cookin' At Norma's House?

*"Relatively" speaking, Norma is my first cousin. We go back to a time when cousins
were raised in close family relationships and we all enjoyed reunions where
everyone brought a dish to pass and a copy of their recipe was always being
requested. Now in the retirement years the miles have come between us, but the
love in relationships remains. Check out this mouth watering recipe she gave me
many years ago. I think you'll like it!*

SERVES 4

1 med. onion coarsely chopped

1 package (10 oz) frozen mixed vegetables - thawed

1/2 cup cider vinegar

1/3 cup water

3 tbsp sugar

1/2 tsp mustard seed

1/2 tsp salt

* * *

*(Salt note; Salt enhances sweet flavors. Proper function of salt is to develop and
bring out natural food flavors, not to make foods taste salty. Sprinkle small amount
on or in fruit juices. It increases sourness of acids and increases sweetness of
sugars.)*

2001 Household Hints and Dollar Stretchers copyright@1957

* * *

1/8 tsp hot pepper sauce

In 2 cup jar or small bowl, mix onion & vegetables. Set aside.

In small pan boil vinegar, water, salt, sugar, mustard seed & hot sauce.

Reduce heat. Simmer 5 minutes. Pour over vegetables.

Cover and refrigerate at least 2 hours before serving.

Surprise Seasoning Blend
Another recipe from the kitchen of my Mother's friend...."Toots"

1 Tbsp each of the following;

Salt

Pepper

Onion Powder

Garlic powder

Oregano

Thyme

Parsley

Paprika

Put in layers in a glass jar. Shake until mixed.

Use for salads, stews, popcorn, chip dips, veggie dips etc.

(Add 1 tsp to 1/2 cup mayonnaise for using as salad dressing)

Friendship Tea

From the recipe memories of my Mother's friend...

Violet "Toots" DeNio

2 Cups Tang

1/2 Cup instant tea

1 tsp cinnamon

1 tsp ground cloves

1 1/2 sugar-optional

1 pkg Lemonade mix..unsweetened.

USE 1/2 TSP.   OF ABOVE MIX OR MORE TO TASTE - TO 1
CUP BOILING WATER

*You may acquire so many new friendships with this lovely offering, you'll
have to bake some cookies.*

Mary Gall's Fabulous Caramel Corn

A lovely lady, a great cook and just the tantalizing recipe for which you've been searching. . I haven't tried this one, but I'm getting hungry just looking at the possibilities.

6 quarts Pop Corn (no hard kernels)

Melt 2 sticks margerine

2 Cups Brown Sugar

1/2 Cup White Corn Syrup

1 tsp salt

Bring to boil, stirring constantly to soft ball stage....add 1/2 tsp. Baking Soda, 1 tsp. Vanilla...Pour mixture over popcorn...mix.

Bake at 250 deg. 1 hour in 2 large shallow pans. STIR EVERY 15 MINUTES.

House and Senate Bean Soup
No Subpoena Required

Found these in a newspaper article from a 1987 clipping. I've read and reread. I know there's a message in here somewhere. There seems to be an aroma of truth.

HOUSE

2 pounds number 1 white Michigan beans

1 smoked ham hock

Water

Salt and Pepper to taste

Cover beans with cold water; soak overnight. Drain. Recover with water. Add ham hock simmer slowly about 4 hours until beans are cooked tender. Add salt and pepper to suit taste.

Just before serving, bruise beans with large spoon or ladle, enough to cloud.

Serves about 6 persons.

. . . .

SENATE

1 pound dry navy beans

1 meat ham bone or 1   1/2 pounds ham hocks

1 cup chopped onion

2 garlic cloves, minced

1 cup celery

1 1/2 cups mashed potatoes*

1/4 cup chopped parsley

1 1/2 tsp salt

1 tsp pepper

1 tsp nutmeg

1 tsp oregano

1 tsp basil

1 bay leaf

Two-thirds cup mashed potato flakes may be substituted.

Wash and sort beans.   In large kettle, cover beans with 6 to 8 cups hot water.
Bring to a boil.   Remove from heat, cover and let stand 1 hour.   Add another 2
quarts cold water and ham bone.   Bring to boil, simmer 1 1/2 hours.   Stir in
remaining ingredients.   Simmer 20 to 30 minutes until beans are tender.   Remove
ham bone, trim off meat, return to soup.   Serve hot.   Freeze any leftovers if
desired.

Makes about 3 quarts.

* * * * * *

Dixie's Deviled Chicken
(You could call it Dixie's chicks)

My friend Dixie and I met in a 60+ Chatroom in 1998. We've been internet friends ever since. She is a lovely lady and a great cook from what I hear, but for me, that's not as important as the wonderful friendship between us. Thank heaven for the internet. One of us is living in Florida and one in Michigan, meeting once in Oklahoma face to face in the nineties when my family was on a trip through the West. Many friends were made during the chatroom experience which lasted over a ten year period. As the years go by, it pays to try some of the new inventions...maybe you should try Dixie's recipe too. (She got it originally from the Rachel Ray show. There goes that internet again.)

TOTAL TIME 30 MIN

ACTIVE 30 MIN

YIELD 4 SERVINGS

LEVEL EASY

INGREDIENTS

4 pieces boneless, skinless chicken breast (no tenders)

Salt and Pepper

AP flour, about 1 cup

3 Large Eggs

1 scant tbsp Dijon mustard

3 tbsp milk

3 tbsp Pecorino Romano (Various cheeses of Italian origin made from sheep's milk) or Parmigiano-Reggiano cheese

1/4 to 1/3 cup olive oil or vegetable oil (light in color olive oil or safflower oil)

2 lemons

3 tbsp butter

2 large cloves garlic, 1 crushed or chopped, 1 halved

About 3/4 cup white wine

1 tbsp Calabrian chili paste, harissa or sriracha

About 1 1/2 cups chicken stock

A handful flat-leave parsley, for serving

1 loaf ciabatta bread, 12 to 14 inches long, halved

EVOO, for drizzling (extra virgin olive oil)

Flaky sea salt, for sprinkling

1 large bundle arugula, cleaned, or boxed leaves

1. Gather your ingredients and a gel board to prepare chicken.
2. Halve the chicken breasts horizontally and butterfly them. Use a mallet to thin meat or even it out if needed–it depends on the size of the chicken breasts. Season meat with salt and pepper.
3.Set a station up: Flour in shallow dish; eggs beaten with

mustard, milk, salt, pepper and cheese; large frying pan with oil (4 to 5 turns of the pan); a baking sheet with wire rack inserted and lined with parchment paper to remove the chicken to.
4. Preheat the oil in skillet over medium to medium-high heat. Coat chicken 2 at a time in flour, shake off excess to drip off. Cook chicken 3-4 minutes on each side. Repeat, removing cooked chicken to wire rack. Once chicken is cooked, slice and lightly brown 1 lemon; add to pan with chicken. Wipe excess oil from pan, return to heat and add butter. When it foams add 1 clove crushed garlic, juice of 1 lemon, wine and chili paste and reduce abut 3 minutes. Add stock and reduce 5 minutes more. Pick and chop the parsley.
5. Char the bread over gas burner or under broiler. Rub charred bread with halved garlic, drizzle with EVOO, sprinkle with flaky sea salt and cut bread into chunks.
6. Add the chicken back to sauce and heat the meat, through, 3-4 minutes, turning occasionally. Add the sliced lemons and coat with sauce. Add parsley and transfer to plates. Serve cutlets with a small handful of arugula leaves alongside and some charred bread for mopping.

Nickie's Down Home Spaghetti Sauce

Visiting friends in Ohio when Nickie shared her wonderful spaghetti recipe with us. Simply done, smells great while it's cooking and tastes unbelievably good when we can it and use it throughout the year.

40 bush tomatoes (approximately) run thru blender

12 medium onions (run thru blender)

6 green peppers (run thru blender)

Cook down and add

2 TBLSp Basil

2 TBLSp Oregano

2 TBLSp Parsley

16 oz vegetable oil

2TBLSp garlic

1 cup sugar

1/4 cup salt

Cook some more...then can it

Makes 8 qts

Folks used to can for the winter months every year. Some still do and it takes us back to the days of Mom and Grandma and the great smell in the house while preparations are underway.

About the Author

Since high school, Mary Anne has enjoyed writing about experiences she's had, the places she's been, people she has known. In her late twenties, married with two kids and another on the way, she was offered the opportunity to write for the local newspaper. The subject was hers to choose, the title was chosen by the editor; "Musings of A Homemaker", readers were invited to share recipes to be printed at the end of her articles. She has included them in her book along with recipes that have a home in her kitchen cupboard recipe box as it sits on the shelf.

She has shared experiences of her Christian walk, the family, patriotic moments of reflection, and friendships. A little humor is good for the soul, and that's included along with an opinion or two. As her friends often tell her, "You always have a story".

They're right she does.

Printed in the USA
CPSIA information can be obtained
at www.ICGtesting.com
CBHW021331231124
17916CB00010B/168